My Speaking Journey

by

Gwyn Redgers

To Lis

With best wishes,

Gwyn

Published in UK in 2015
Published by Gwyn Redgers
ISBN 978-0-9934363-0-7
Printed in Great Britain by Stroma Ltd

With thanks to Tony Coleman, Tony Scott, editors
of The Speaker and others for illustrations; to
those who helped the author with proof-reading
and editing advice; to Caroline Brown for design;
and to staff at Stroma Publishing Ltd.

Table of Contents

Preface

I was at home, tidying up my filing system, when I found a copy of 'The Speaker' magazine from the year 1980. This was the year that I first came across ASC – the Association of Speakers Clubs. Reading through that magazine I noticed that a new Archive Officer had been appointed, namely Maurice Scott-Dodd. In a very brief article, he had stated that one of his post's purposes was to keep important ASC documents on file until such time in the future as someone chose to write the history of the ASC.

It is not my intention to write such a history, whether formal or informal. However these words gave me the idea of committing to paper (or to my computer, as we do nowadays) the story of my own personal journey within the ASC. After all, nearly 35 years of membership is no mean feat.

Naturally I can only really include aspects in which I have been personally involved. For example the very important history of ASC in Scotland will certainly require a different author. However I was fortunate enough to have had the opportunity, as time went on, to develop a wider involvement within the organisation, which I have tried to convey in these chapters.

Also as time went on I branched out into a broader range of speaking activities, especially including debating. These too are very much a part of my speaking journey but, to keep focus on my ASC journey, I have covered all these non-ASC activities together in a final chapter.

The views which I write are my personal views and do not in any way represent those of the Association. Also I should apologise for the errors which I shall certainly make as I write, and for the lapses of memory and my own gaps in records.

Finally my thanks go out to all those ASC members and others who have helped me on every step of the way and whose friendship I have enjoyed and continue to enjoy.

Chapter 1

The Start of the Journey

It was one evening in late 1980 that Julie came home, described her afternoon and told me that she had been talking to Tom Williams of GCHQ. "He was telling me about a new speakers club that has been started. 'My husband might be interested in that', I told him". And so it was that one February evening in 1981 I went along as a visitor to my first speakers club meeting.

That particular meeting was held in the George Hotel near the centre of Cheltenham. I recall that there were some 10 or 11 people in the room. All of us were men, of course, at that time. The event was a joint meeting with a speakers club from Cardiff. A chap called Chris Austen, Cheltenham's President, chaired the meeting, two or three of those present gave fairly short speeches, followed by comments which I understood were called 'evaluations'. Then, following a fairly short interval to fill up our glasses, all present had a go at speaking for just two minutes. I was asked, if I remember rightly (34 years later), to talk about my favourite type of holiday. One of the Cardiff visitors present gave some comments on my talk, which were quite encouraging, I recall. Then, fairly soon after this, the meeting ended.

It had been a totally new experience for me, quite unexpected in various ways. However I realised that I now had a decision to make. Should I or should I not join this "Cheltenham Speakers Club"? It had at that time just seven or eight members. I felt that it would be unfair to them to simply play at it. Either I should become a member and attend regularly. Or I should not go again and not waste their time.

In fact the decision was for me quite an easy one to make. Within my company, I had recently been asked to go out once a month to meetings of the local sales groups, and to give a talk. This was totally new ground for me. It was clear to me, from the meeting which I had just attended, that I could do with the skills and experience which the speakers club would provide. The evaluation of my two-minute topics talk in particular had convinced me of this. And thus, in early 1981, I took the plunge and became a speakers club member.

It seems strange, looking back, to realise how distant I had been from speaking until I was in my 40s. In my grammar school in Enfield, I had been an active participant in school clubs, but the question of improving speaking skills had never cropped up. (In fact it would take another 20 or more years before the question of learning speaking at school first became a live issue, and it is still quite a rarity) Then, after National Service, came my university years at Trinity, Cambridge. Once again, this was an extremely active period for me, which included running rag-days and being a member of a number of societies. I was even a regular (though silent) attendee at many stirring debates in the Cambridge Union. My working career began with several years in a large American advertising agency in London, which was followed by a few years of product management in the consumer goods field. Then finally I had become one of the early pioneers of the still newish discipline of 'marketing' in the financial services world.

It was in 1977 that a career opportunity with a life assurance company took me away from the City of London to the beauty of the Cotswolds.

The life assurance world was still very dependent on speaking, whether this was the salesman's gift of the gab or, at times, the inspiring words of a motivational platform speaker. Once or twice I had needed to speak at sales conferences, and am pleased to say that I felt that I did not let the side down. Our HR department had also arranged for some of us a 1-day speaking course from an outside consultant. I can still remember the comment made to me by that tutor on that day. "You speak quite well, Mr Redgers, and have a good voice. But why on earth do you keep moving forward and back when you're speaking?" So perhaps I was ready for the speakers club opportunity when it arrived.

This speakers club had actually been founded a couple of years before. It was originally started in the nearby town of Tewkesbury and bore the name of Tewkesbury Speakers Club. This was slightly nearer to Stourbridge, whose speakers club had started our club. However it had now transferred to Cheltenham, meeting firstly in the function room of a local public house and then in the Sports & Social Club of the large local employer, Dowty's. The club's President for those first few years was Chris Austen, and Julie's friend Tom Williams was the club's Secretary.

My memories of those early days of speakers club life are pleasant ones. As a new paid-up member, I received my copy of the Manual as it was then normally called (later to be renamed the Speakers Guide). At each meeting, I would take part in the Topics session of impromptu speaking, and duly received comments from an evaluator. I recall that in those first two or three months, I performed my Icebreaker speech, and went on to the 'mean what you say' assignment, the 'speech construction' assignment and the 'gestures' assignment. I was starting to find my voice.

Just as importantly, I was starting to find a new circle of friends. It had not occurred to me, when I took that initial plunge and started learning and practising, that friendships would also develop. But, as I was to find out constantly over these years of membership, speakers clubs provide considerable social benefit and pleasure also. Those who attend speakers clubs seem nearly always to be friendly and interesting people. What starts off as a "shared learning" liaison turns without realising it into the friendship relationships that you get from a good club. To this day I retain one or two of those early fellow-members on my regular Christmas Card list, despite the fact that 34 years have since passed.

Continuing my personal story, I was a keen enough member to accept the office of Club Secretary in my second year, 1981/1982, and thereby started to receive correspondence from the wider Association. After all, it was still several years before emails and the spread of the Internet were to change administration methods profoundly. An early and always popular arrival were the copies of "The Speaker", which arrived in bulk and were duly passed around both members and possibly also to visitors.

These, together with the mailings from the National Secretary, were an indication there was more to ASC life then simply our own club. More immediately, however, the importance of Area started to emerge. Cheltenham was part of the Midlands District's 'West Midlands Area' which at that time consisted also of Stourbridge, Solihull, South Warwicks and Sutton Coldfield. One of my early away trips was to Solihull club, which gave me the chance to meet and learn from, amongst others, Walter Hewson, who was certainly the District's leading marketing figure at that time. Another visit was to our parent club at Stourbridge. This was my first encounter with Dilwyn Scott who, I see from that evening's programme, evaluated the speech that I gave on that occasion. Dilwyn's father, Coulson Scott, had been one of the leading members at the time in late 1971 that ASC broke free from the international Toastmasters organisation and became its own independent entity. Dilwyn, of course, went on to become a leading figure in ASC in his own right, not merely as a long serving national officer and as National President in 2000, but also as a speaking trainer and as a constitutional expert always ready to help guide the business of every AGM.

As well as simple club visits – home or away – the Midlands District clubs had developed a pattern of competitive team events. For instance Solihull had its Spouters Stump competition and Wolverhampton had its Gabbers Gear competition. A theme would have been notified in advance and then, on the date, each club's team of three or four members – possibly with some supporters – would assemble and enjoy some friendly rivalry. Each team (that is perhaps one chairman and 3 members) would give speeches on the theme. One of the earlier ones that I still remember well was a Spouters Stump contest in which the theme was "The Victorians". I recall that my own speech bore the title "A Victorian Obsession", and dealt with the fascination with death and funerals in those years. Cheltenham's other team members dealt with 'empire building' and with 'Isambard Kingdom Brunel', and we came away with the trophy.

It was in April 1982, towards the close of that first year as Club Secretary, that Chris Austen, our President, and I decided that we should go to the National Conference as day-trippers. It was being held that year in Harrogate. My main memory of that day was the professionalism of the General Council meeting itself. Running the meeting was National President Jarvis Scott. He proved to be completely in command of the business meeting, and also enlivened it with brief snatches of wit. I had already been told that one of the benefits of attending a speakers club was that it gave good experience and instruction on chairing meetings. That morning I saw it for myself. Chris and I attended an afternoon seminar and the speech contest final, and then drove back to Cheltenham, but the memory of that first AGM still lingers on.

It also inspired me to become a regular attendee at National Conference. I can only recall missing one National Conference in all the years that have followed.

Cheltenham Speakers Club, however, still remained small. We still had some way to go to reach the figure of 16 or 17 members which, I believe, was the average size of speakers clubs at that time. During our next committee meeting, Tom Williams mentioned a conversation which he had held a few months earlier with Harry Hislop of Cardiff Speakers Club. This was about a speaking course which Cardiff had run to help build its numbers. Could this be our route too, we asked ourselves? We decided there and then that we should try this method, and I found myself with the task of organising it. This was an important milestone in my personal speakers club career, and one I have never regretted.

The first task was to find out more and if possible get the details of the Cardiff course. This was very necessary since I had barely reached the halfway stage myself in working through the Manual. My attempt to run a speaking course reminded me of an incident from many years before, at school in Enfield, when several of us in the fifth form were given the opportunity to learn Spanish. The only problem was the lack of a Spanish teacher. This problem was solved by a French teacher, Mr Hudson, volunteering to teach us from the start of a grammar book whilst he was still learning Spanish from the final pages of that same grammar book. I felt myself to be in a similar position in attempting to train others in speaking whilst still at an early stage. However I did have some useful teaching experience – albeit in a totally different subject – since I had run a Spanish evening course for two or three years when I was first married and badly needed the money

Possibly the most important factor, and one which we got right from the outset, was the scheduling. We would run the course on the same night as club meetings. It would last for one and a half hours before the club meeting.

This not only eased the room-booking problem, but also meant that those who attended the course would be able, if they wished, to stay on for the main club meeting. We also decided that the final meeting of the course programme, in which course members would give their final speech and would receive a certificate, should be a joint meeting with the club itself. These are quite possibly the principal factors that have led to the great recruiting success of the many pre-meeting courses that I and others have held since those early days.

The course, and also the club meetings, would be starting in September. A press release was sent to the local paper, and specially prepared leaflets were put in hand. A particularly significant factor then took place. I provided a pile of club leaflets and a pile of course leaflets to the local library, which put both on display. Three days later I returned to the library and discovered that, whereas some club leaflets were still on the counter, all the course leaflets had been taken in the first two days. This was my own first realisation of a basic truth about speakers club recruitment that now seems obvious. Easily the main reason why people join a speakers club is to get some training, and clearly that was the message of the course leaflet. The appeal of joining a club is significantly less.

We were very pleased at the results. Some eight or nine people signed up, attended the six sessions, and eventually gained their certificate. This provided the club with clear benefits. Firstly it received some £90 in course fees. Secondly the club now appeared stronger in spirit and had a good story to tell to the community. Thirdly, two or three of the course attendees became members of Cheltenham Speakers Club.

Over the years this pattern has repeated itself every time that I or others have run this type of course in speakers clubs. On average, about one third of attendees will decide to continue with the club. Numbers can readily be built up this way. Also it will compensate a more established club for the fact that two or three of its members are always very likely to leave in a year. Over the years I continue to look with amazement at how few speakers clubs use the pre-meeting course method to build or keep up their numbers.

My own experience continued to grow. Given my career in marketing, it is not surprising that my memory of those days is strongest for some new club aspects. ASC had developed from Scotland and the North, and was moving southwards. At that time, south western development beyond Cheltenham had barely started. In fact the only ASC club (other than in South Wales) was the Moonrakers Speakers Club in Devizes. Discussions began about starting a speakers club in Swindon. Naturally we at Cheltenham would give whatever support we could.

The launch event was not auspicious. About a dozen people attended the opening meeting, but only one of these was a Swindon resident, Andy Goodhead. The others came from Cheltenham and Devizes, with the addition of a Scotsman who had travelled down from Perth for that occasion. However, thanks to the keenness and perseverance of Andy and one or two local members, Swindon Speakers Club developed fairly soon into a strong and lively speakers club. Many years later, I was privileged to have the opportunity of speaking at the club's 25th anniversary dinner, and of recalling that initial meeting.

And that visitor from Scotland? This was none other than Ken Lewison who was for numerous years the National Secretary of ASC and who went on to become a renowned Life Member. He had spent time in Swindon in his early years, where his father was a deputy to the GWR's great mechanical engineer, Churchward, and was thus based in Swindon. Ken and I were to spend many hours together as time went on, and his name will crop up several times within these chapters.

Another development taking place in those very early years concerned the female side of speaking. ASC was certainly not the only organisation which started off as 'men only' and later widened to cover both sexes. It was very specifically a male organisation in its early years. At the same time, quite a number of Ladies Speakers Clubs had been established in various parts of the country. These were organised into several 'Ladies Councils' and were affiliated to the ASC. Thus, at the start of my time in the speakers club movement, the only method open for a go-ahead speakers club was to start a separate ladies club. "Mixed" clubs were still in the future.

The urgent need for action on this front was brought home to me whilst seeking press publicity for the Cheltenham club's new speaking course. As a result of sending a press release to the Gloucestershire Echo, I agreed to be interviewed at home. A fairly young female journalist arrived one Saturday morning, armed with pen and pad, and the interview started. Why was the speakers club putting on a course? What would the course consist of? Where would it be held? And what about the speakers club itself – How long had it been running? What did it do? How many members? Was there any difference between the male and female members? At that point I informed the reporter that the club was for men only. Horrified, she stopped the interview, put pen and pad back in her bag, and left the house.

Fortunately one or two of us had female friends who were potentially interested in a ladies speakers club. Quite soon, Cheltenham Ladies Speakers Club was established and meetings started to be held. The club affiliated to Ladies Council No. 3 which extended from the West Midlands right across the country to Dover! This new club, in its turn, introduced members such as Pamela Chance who would go on to play a significant role in the future in ASC. However there was one risky moment.

This was the occasion when a highly skilled ASC Area President, Barry Picken, was invited by the Ladies Club to attend its meeting and to give the general evaluation. He duly did so. Much to our surprise we learned shortly after that meeting that the ladies club had lost two or possibly three of its members as a result of Barry's full and forthright evaluation. The evaluator's comments on their speeches had been interpreted by some of the ladies present as evaluation – not of the speech – but of the person making the speech. I remember talking a few days later to one of the departed members who asked me, somewhat saddened, "Why didn't he like me?" Another valuable lesson had been learned.

Meanwhile I moved from the position of Club Secretary to Education Officer and then, in 1984, had the privilege of becoming President of the club. Overall the Cheltenham Speakers Club continued to proceed well. We enjoyed our speaking, and were progressing. Meetings and visits were made. We decided that our club too should have an event in which members of other clubs could take part. The result was the launch of the Severn Bore annual topics contest, with Chepstow (which is on the River Severn) as the venue and Cardiff Speakers Club as one of the several other clubs involved. Two or three years later, the Cheltenham club created the Cheltenham Hurdle team-speaking event for clubs in the local area. However the Severn Bore Topics Contest continued in that format for quite a few further years.

Our social programme in the year when I was Club President also included an enjoyable evening in the famous Speech House in the Forest of Dean. To mark the occasion we held a Mock Trial of a scoundrel who had not only poached the King's deer, but had also run away with the Lord of the Manor's daughter. He was duly sentenced by Tom Williams, who was 'wearing the wig' that evening.

Mention of Tom Williams reminds me that I may well hold a unique position amongst ASC's club presidents. The fact is that half of my committee had taken a vow of silence. The clue is, of course, the location – 'Cheltenham' – which is home to GCHQ. Very often a new member's icebreaker speech will include telling us about his or her professional employment. This of course was not forthcoming from our GCHQ members. Tom Williams was just one of the GCHQ employees who played an important part in the club's life. Of course we never knew the details of his employment activity. It was only after the event that we might hear by chance that Tom had just been to New York or possibly to Cyprus. Another was Steve Wilkie, who became Club President for a year later on. His name actually appeared in the local paper since he was closely concerned in the non-secret attempt by some GCHQ employees to gain permission for trade union activity.

Another memory of my year as Club President concerned our annual dinner, where I had as a personal guest the chief executive of Cheltenham's local radio station, Eddie Vickers, whom I knew well from my work. Another person whom I had invited to the dinner was Len Mears, also from the Midlands District, who was now National President. By this time I had met both him and his wife on several occasions, so I sent an invitation letter to 'Len and Dorothy'. I still have his letter of response. "Dear Gwyn, I would like to bring Dorothy with me, but I guess that I had better bring Barbara who is my one and only wife". This was unfortunately not the last time that I have got a name wrong!

For me personally my year as Club President ended in an unexpected way.

This was the invitation by West Midlands Area President, Ron Sutton, to take over from him as Area President for the following year. My speakers club life had started to spread beyond the confines of just my own club.

Chapter 2

A Wider Role

For any member of a speakers club, the central focus will always be one's own club. It is there that one has the closest friendships and the experience of developing as a speaker. However I really enjoyed my year as Area President of West Midlands Area. I would go as far as to say that the most fulfilling role that anyone can have within ASC is to be an Area President. On one hand, you become very close to your clubs and the people within them. On the other hand you start to build the link with the wider ASC world.

There are good sources of written guidance for the role. Also, in most cases (though not in mine) the incoming Area President is likely to have first spent a year as Area Vice-President, and thus have learned some of the ropes and met some of the people.

A quick summary of the role would be the following. Frequent contact with – and help for – one's clubs by telephone or other means. Occasionally visiting one's clubs on a club night or perhaps at their dinner, and taking on a role. Holding Area Council meetings plus the Area's annual AGM and contest meeting. Quite possibly arranging and running a seminar during one's year. If possible, assisting in new club development within the Area. Plus, of course, being a channel of communication from club to District and vice-versa, and playing one's part fully in the District Council.

Much time has passed since the year 1985/1986, and I no longer have the day to day records of visits and meetings. However memories remain fresh. For example, the people whom I met. There were those members from Stourbridge who had been the godparents of my own club. One who had been particularly influential in starting our club was the elderly Dennis Pauli who had earlier used the same speech therapist that King George VI had used. There were senior figures who I have already mentioned, such as Dilwyn Scott and Walter Hewson. There was Barry Picken, who was holding a speaking course in Foley and starting to turn it into a speakers club. Alan Hunter, my Area Vice-President, and South Warwicks Club's Joe Davis could always be relied on to help in clubs nearer to Birmingham. I remember particularly one evening when Joe was general evaluator and completely (and rightly) overturned the verdicts of two speech evaluators. Yes, some members in those days took no hostages!

Possibly even more important than any of these was the Midlands District President, Bob Tebbett, who was always on hand to assist and advise.

I might well be asked, when I visited a club, to take on the role of General Evaluator. Also, at times, I might be asked to give a tutorial. After all, every club must never forget that training in speaking should be at the core of their activity. With my growing experience of speaking courses behind me, I had started to put together tutorials for, say, 10-15 minutes on some of the main aspects of public speaking. (Looking at my files quite recently, I discovered to my surprise that I have accumulated a list of almost 30 tutorials which I could still give!)

It was the pattern at that time in Midlands District – certainly in the West Midlands Area – for an Area President to hold a seminar during his year of office. There were several possibilities, and in the end I decided that my seminar would be on the subject of Judging Contests. I had now had enough experience of judging speech and evaluation contests (there were no topics contests until a few years later!) to realise that some expert guidance was needed, especially by those judging for the first time. The judging form is provided, showing the marks available under six or seven headings, but surely there must be a best way of filling it in. Len Mears, by now an ex-National President, was once again willing to help by passing on his judging skills and experience to us all. It was in this seminar that I learned for the first time the common sense approach of starting with scores close to the medium level, and the usefulness of dividing a category into, say, 4 specific items – each with 5 points – rather than leaving it as an overall 'marks out of 20' category. I also appreciated the advice to enter the various scores as the speech proceeded, probably leaving to the end only the marks for the conclusion and for the overall impression. It was certainly a highly useful seminar, and one which Len and I were asked to repeat a year or two later at National Conference.

But quite probably the most significant activity which I undertook during my year of office was to seek to develop new clubs. After all, I was a marketing executive in my day job, so this was a natural wish.

ASC at that point was definitely in a growth phase and growth mood. As I briefly mentioned earlier, ASC had sprung from Toastmasters clubs, which had first arrived in this country from America in the mid-30s. They had initially become established in Scotland. Then, during the post-war period and by the time of the defection from Toastmasters in 1971, they had spread widely over the North of England, the Midlands, and on to the first pioneering clubs mainly in the south-east. However this left huge areas towards the south of the country, plus of course numerous towns, still without a speakers club. The requirement was obvious. The population as a whole needed to have the opportunity to learn public speaking, and there was no better way than through a speakers club. The task for ASC was to set up these clubs. And who better than the Area President to take a lead in that task?

The situation that I inherited as Area President of the West Midlands Area was that we had 5 clubs (all male, of course). As already mentioned, these were Cheltenham, Solihull, Stourbridge, South Warwicks and Sutton Coldfield. In addition there was the Cheltenham Ladies Speakers Club, and the embryo club being put together by Barry Picken in Foley.

With all the naiveté of a new person starting out, I decided that my target should be to try to double the number from 5 to 10 in my year of Area office.

The general assumption at that time, which quite probably still exists, is that a new speakers club will be started by an existing speakers club. After all, that was the way in which my own club, Cheltenham, had been established. It quickly became clear that this would not be the way to achieve my own ambitious target. I had a supportive Area Council. However it is only natural that members of speakers clubs think first of all – and quite possibly only – of the success of their own club, and only occasionally have interest in starting a new club. Indeed, some members will be worried that starting a new club fairly nearby might even jeopardise their own club's growth.

So if I were to achieve my aim of doubling the number of clubs, another method had to be found. The one I chose was, firstly, to find people in a target town who would like to have a speakers club there and, secondly, to build the club around them. Fortunately I was not alone in this task because I had with me my Area Vice-President, Alan Hunter, and also a colleague from my office – Pam Sewell – who was at that time the local leader of the Ladies Council No 3 speakers clubs.

The first step was to decide which towns to aim for. I therefore created a map which showed the location of the existing 5 clubs and picked out other centres of population which as yet had no club. I chose about 10 of these within the accepted West Midlands area, ranging from Coventry down to Witney and including such places as Worcester to the west, and Banbury and Bicester to the east.

The next step was to send a letter to the local Press and also to the libraries in those locations. The basic message was a fairly simple one. "Speakers clubs are the popular way in which thousands of people are learning public speaking. However there is not yet one in (name of town). Please get in touch if you would be interested in having one in (name of town)." These letters, if published, each tended to produce about three or four replies of varying potential. I recall one from the President of a Toastmasters Club in Oxford, who was very wary about a competitor setting up fairly nearby in Witney. (I was aware that half a dozen Toastmasters clubs had not switched to ASC, and still existed in the southern counties, but his phone call was my first contact with any of them!) Another reply came from a speech training company, and was equally wary of our attempt to provide a rival method of learning.

The third step, often much trickier than it sounds, was to set up an informal meeting, normally in a pub, with these 3 or 4 people from a given town. I was able to do this, in Malvern, Daventry, Bicester and Witney whilst possibilities also emerged from a speaking training course held near Dudley and an independent club in Coventry.

My personal agenda for these meetings was similar in every case. Most of those whom I met had never heard of a speakers club. The initial task was to explain all about them – where they were, what they did, how they were organised – and answer questions. I would then look for some form of commitment to start the process.

It would be for the locals to run the club as President, Secretary, Treasurer and so on. It would also be for the locals to find and decide on a venue (absolutely necessary) and fix a date for commencing. This might take the form of an open meeting, a first club meeting, or even a course. Meanwhile I or an ASC colleague would come on to their new committee as Education Officer, and thus provide the missing elements of speaking training knowledge, and programme planning. In addition members of other local clubs in the Area would take care of the evaluations in those early meetings.

Not everything succeeded of course. Some whom I met hesitated to become involved. At times it was hard to pin down people to carry out actions or even to communicate. A social club in Coventry which, for a time, was the most promising of all, finally decided to stay independent. However we did succeed in holding initial club meetings or open meetings in Witney, Malvern and Daventry. In addition the Foley Speakers Club development was proceeding, some who had contacted me as a result of my letter to Evesham decided instead to join the Malvern venture, and the efforts of Pam Sewell and especially of Pamela Chance led to the successful launch of Gloucester Speakers Club.

There were slices of luck too. For instance, the organiser of a "Soapbox Club" near the airbase of Carterton heard about what was being planned in Witney and suggested that we joined forces. His name was Ernie Crapper and, yes, he really was the great-great-grandson of that Victorian inventor of the present-day toilet flush. He and his members did join the new Witney Speakers Club, and this led to a most successful club for several years. Incidentally it also led to Witney resident Pat Reeve joining the Association 3 or 4 years later, and eventually taking on the role of South Western District President. Pat sadly died about 10 years ago. However her husband John kindly created the 'Pat Reeve Bursary' specifically for the District's representative in the National speech contest.

All in all, the new club openings could be counted as quite a satisfactory result to what had been an extraordinarily busy year. There were definitely lessons to be learned. Those that have stayed with me include:

(i)   the vital importance of getting a venue and fixing a date for an opening meeting right from the start. The planning can then run smoothly from that start.

(ii)   the need to have meeting routines of high standard right from the outset, and also a 'role model' present if you expect the visitors to see the point of joining

(iii) the feasibility and advantages of empowering the local committee to plan and run their show (with an experienced Education Officer from outside to assist and provide the knowledge and evaluators)

(iv) the willingness of people from a local club to carry out evaluations and roles at the new club, and thus get it fully self-supporting in about 6 meetings.

At the end of my year as Area President, I wrote up a full report of this new club experiment, and circulated it to the other Areas within the Midlands district and also to ASC's national body – the NEC (National Executive Council).

One important issue had to be faced. Each of these new clubs had mixed male and female membership. Yes, they all wished to become a fully chartered Speakers Club (and all but one eventually did so), but the rules of the Association would need to be changed first. So far attempts to allow mixed-sex clubs had failed to elicit the necessary two-thirds support from General Council at the Annual Conference. The weight of opinion, especially in the Scottish heartlands of the Association, was still seeing ASC as exclusively a men's organisation. Hopefully this could be ended. The position of women in the country and in the workforce was rapidly changing, and women's needs for what ASC could offer were now as great as men's needs. The previous solution, i.e. meeting women's needs only by having separate speakers clubs for women, was certainly no longer the answer.

In fact there were even those radicals who suggested that we would have to become independent of ASC unless rules were changed. The battle lines were being drawn.

It was also clear that I personally might become involved in this. The reason was that I had accepted nomination for the following year, 1986/1987, as District Vice-President of Midlands District, and had been voted into this office at the District's annual meeting. Taking office at District level would be a different challenge and, with that year of Area office behind me, I looked forward to it.

The main role of the District Vice-President within ASC is to learn the ropes of the job, and to meet the clubs and the people, ready for the time when he or she takes over the role of District President. I was pleased that, by the time that I took over this role in 1986, I had already met quite a number of the Midlands people. This was partly through attendance at the District Council meetings and the National Conferences which I had been attending each year. It was also through other events.

I recall with pleasure, for instance, the Dinner in the House of Commons to celebrate the 25th year of Wolverhampton Speakers Club. Such an event is required to have a member one of the two Houses of Parliament as the host. Our host on that occasion was Roger King MP who had been the President of Wolverhampton Speakers Club before being elected as an MP. It was a memorable occasion. Incidentally, just a few years later, Roger King himself readily agreed to imagine himself still an ASC member and to give the Toast to the Guests at the Speaker of the Year Dinner for Betty Boothroyd (now 'Dame') who was then the Speaker of the House of Commons. (The reply from the guests was given by Tony Benn MP.) Roger recalled with fondness his ASC days and also expounded most interestingly on the subject of 'soundbites'. The 2-minute Topic speech which we practise in speakers club meetings is certainly worthwhile. However if we are suddenly stopped in the road by a journalist or TV reporter and are asked to give a view, we need to give the clearest possible message in no more than a 15 to 30 second "soundbite".

Another and slightly less joyous memory for me was an excellent annual dinner which I had attended at the Moonrakers Speakers Club in Devizes. The Moonrakers President decided, unusually, to include a topics session as after-dinner entertainment. Being a visitor from another club, I was kindly invited to take part. The topic given to me was "public speaking" and, for possibly the only time in my life, I dried up. As I say, that evening was slightly less joyous for me, but it certainly brought home to me the difficulty often faced by visitors doing topics for the first time.

Now, as District Vice-President, I would need to get to know the whole District better. Midlands District was very far-flung. It currently extended from Devizes in the south to Cardiff in the west and to Stafford and Derby at the northern end. Moreover expansion was in the air. Towards the south, Bath and Bristol were being considered, and also the possibility of Salisbury. To the east, a club was being planned for Lincoln. To the west, Harry Hislop and Dennis Damond-John felt strongly that Wales should have more than just its Cardiff club and were already planning to open first in Barry and then possibly in other South Wales locations.

Then came the news that Southern District, which up to then had consisted of some clubs in East Anglia and Kent, one in Brighton, and a few others mainly in Greater London, was considering starting a club in Bournemouth (probably to be called the 'Westbourne Speakers Club') or even further into Dorset.

To us in Cheltenham it was clear that, if there were to be a new club in Bournemouth, it would be far better supported by linking it with the southward development from Swindon and Devizes. In fact the whole District structure of ASC needed some rethinking, and discussion should start.

One of the differences in the ASC of almost 30 years ago was that the District Vice-President, as well as the District President, attended the thrice-yearly meetings of the NEC. These were held in Carlisle, and that year's President was Derek Shaw. I found the occasion both enjoyable and workmanlike, and have continued to hold that view in my experience of the NEC in the years that have followed. That year, the Midlands District President, Peter Levy, was allocated by Derek Shaw to the Education Committee, while I was allocated to the NEC's Development Committee. I therefore decided to try and put my own business background to use in respect of the ASC's District structure.

Whether for market research reasons or otherwise, I had frequently needed to work with the Registrar-General's Standard Regions. With the help of these, I prepared a plan based on population areas and on the location of clubs which would provide a better basis for ASC in the Midlands and South. The solution was to create, south of the Midlands District, both a South Western and a South Eastern district. The South Western District would include South Wales and the Cotswolds, Devizes and Swindon, and extend right down to the South Coast. Meanwhile the South Eastern District would go from Milton Keynes and East Anglia, down through London, to Kent and Sussex and possibly as far east as Portsmouth or even Southampton.

The analysis also included the same population and club location data for the four districts north of the Midlands, though without suggesting any changes. My fellow members of the Development Committee discussed this whole proposal and added a further step. This was for Scotland to be divided into three districts instead of the two which then existed. The full plan was agreed by NEC, then in due course by General Council, and became operational in the following year.

The new arrangement however led to one unintended consequence. That was the fact that, with the increase to 8 Districts, there would be no less than 16 District representatives attending NEC meeting each time unless steps were taken. Thus the decision was taken that the District Vice-Presidents would, in future, not normally attend NEC.

More positively, another implication which was gradually realised over time was that a national executive committee consisting of 7 principal National Officers and 8 officers from the Districts was a very suitable ratio.

But then, at the start of 1987 and before I had finished my year as District Vice-President, something happened which would change my own ASC life in a really major way.

A few months earlier, my Gloucester-based employer had been taken over. As so often in these cases, my position in the company's pecking order was thereby worsened. It was time to consider my position. I therefore took the decision, though difficult from a family point of view, to accept a Marketing Director position in the same industry in London. From February 1987, I would be working in London from Monday to Friday and returning home to the Cotswolds for the weekend. Hence I resigned as Midlands District-Vice-

President and handed over to Peter Sterry. From now on, my speakers club life would be in the South East. A new chapter had dawned.

Chapter 3

The Croydon years

Early in 1987, I joined the fairly small life assurance company, Regency Life, as Marketing Director. For the first few months, the office was in Holborn, but quite soon we moved to new premises in Docklands. The area was in the process of being developed to what it has become today. The Docklands Light Railway was running, and some of the highest tower blocks were already in place. But it was still the scene of intense building activity, with more working cranes than I had ever seen previously in my life.

I was fortunate with my accommodation. My aunt and uncle, who had lived in Colliers Wood, South London, since 1927, had just moved into care accommodation and I was able to take over their flat.

Relocating meant being in London and away from the family from Monday to Friday, driving back home to the Cotswolds every Friday evening for the weekend. Additionally, of course, it also meant hunting for a new speakers club to join in London.

By this time in ASC's history, there were several possibilities in South London. Three or four miles to the south-west were a club in Cheam and another – the North Surrey club – near Kingston. Three or four miles to the south-east were Croydon Speakers Club, established 6 or 7 years previously, and two clubs – Fairfield and Whitgift – which had been formed by the Croydon club. All were possibilities. The one that I chose was Croydon Speakers Club itself. One reason was that it was fairly convenient for my new address. Another reason was that I had already met some of the club's members. These included Southern District's Development Officer Brian Worthington whom I had got to know at ASC's national conferences and who was the energetic founder of some of these clubs. We had discussed tactics together when we were trying to get mixed clubs allowed in the Association. In addition I had met Terris Laird at NEC in his earlier role as National Minutes Secretary, and also Geoff Andrews who had been the appointed Convenor of the previous year's National Conference in Shepperton. Croydon proved a good choice in every way and I stayed as a member of the club for the next seven years.

We met in those days upstairs in the Blacksmith's Arms, quite near to central Croydon. Like all the clubs in South Eastern District (apart from West Kent club), it was now becoming a club with both male and female members, though the latter were few in number. The fortnightly programme and the standards of skill were very similar to those that I was used to Cheltenham, and I was able to feel at home straightaway.

From a speaking point of view, I continued working through the Manual from the level I had reached in Cheltenham, and eventually passed my 'masterpiece' level whilst I was a member of Croydon club.

In fact, in my speaking, I was able to go further than I had previously achieved. In 1989, I succeeded in winning the Club, Area and District speech contests and thereby became the South Eastern District's contestant for the National Speech Contest Final. National Conference was held that year in the Lancashire town of Chorley, almost adjacent to the M6 service station of that name. For me it was an anxious occasion. I recall, for instance, opting out of lunch and instead spending considerable time pacing up and down outside in the grounds and practising my speech. My own offering for that contest final was a speech entitled "Spread a little schizophrenia" in which I looked back on some of the great eccentrics of our country, and invited the audience to follow in their path. I was the first of the contenders to give my speech, and enjoyed the experience, but sadly was not a winner. Nevertheless I was proud to have attained that level.

My earlier experience back in Cheltenham (which of course by that time had moved from the Midlands District to the newly-formed South Western District) was useful in several ways. For instance, I had always enjoyed the team-speaking competitions which were such a feature of clubs in that part of the country. These did not yet exist in the south-east, and I was able to introduce the first one. This was the Surrey Shield which was an interclub contest for the clubs south of the Thames. The contest had a pre-announced theme, and involved teams of a chairman and three members. The initiative proved successful and popular. Over time, each of the Areas in the south-east started their own team contest and at least one of these (Kent Area's Hopper Cup) has lasted to the present day.

I was also able to introduce to the Croydon club another speaking activity which had proved most beneficial in the past in the Cheltenham area. This was the pre-meeting 5- or 6-session course, normally held from September to November. During my years at Croydon, I ran this course on 3 or 4 occasions. It was no surprise that it had the same effect of adding 2 or 3 new members to the club each time plus, of course, providing the club with a small but useful amount of revenue.

Ours was certainly not the only speaking course activity in the south-east. A course which was a feature of the District at that time was run for the London branch of the CII (Chartered Insurance Institute). This course had been created initially by ASC member Neil Crichton of Maidstone Speakers Club. The principal trainers during my time at Croydon were Ken Richardson of the Croydon club – later to become District President – and Dennis Carlyle of the Fairfield club – later to become National Development Officer of ASC. I ran various sessions of the course on a number of occasions, and also had the honour of being twice invited to be an Adjudicator for the CII's national speaking contest. It was a great satisfaction to us all that, not only was the course much appreciated by those attending, but also that it evolved into a chartered ASC club – the Insurance Institute Speakers Club.

I have always felt that those speakers club members who have never been beyond the confines of their own club are missing out. Visiting other clubs is a valuable benefit of ASC and is both useful and highly enjoyable. A feature of the speakers club scene in South London at that time was the presence of joint meetings, or simply the ability to travel to another club's meetings quite frequently. The year would be planned to include one (or two) 'Away' trips to another club, and one (or two) 'Home' meetings when we would receive a visit from another club.

One club which I got to know in this way was Horsham Speakers Club. It was Penny Blundell, who was then District Secretary, who told me towards the end of 1989 about this new club. It had just been started by an incomer, Jim Johnston, who had been a member of Nairn Speakers Club and later of a club in Newcastle. I was invited to a meeting of the new club in November 1989, which happened to be only its fourth meeting. The meeting was also attended by an ASC member from Brighton Speakers Club and by one from the Maidstone Ladies Speakers Club. My own role on that occasion was to evaluate the topics session. This was start of a long and happy association, which I shall talk about more fully in later chapters.

There are always highlights – occasions to remember vividly – in one's speakers club life. Perhaps here I can mention two such occasions which stand out from those early years at Croydon.

One of these was due to Croydon member Eric Kings. He was a local councillor with a strong social conscience as well as being a keen member and, later on, the Club President. The highlight to which I refer was the visit that Eric arranged for us to Wandsworth Prison. The purpose was to hold a club vs prisoner debate as part of the prison's education programme for its inmates. The Motion, I recall, was that Britain should become a republic, and six or seven of us from the club went along. I, like anyone else who has ever been inside a prison, have a strong memory of the locking and unlocking of gates and the clanking of large keys. About a dozen inmates joined us for what was a well-prepared debate. Clearly the prisoner who was making the proposal had a deep desire to get rid of the monarchy and had spent some time in careful preparation. The speakers club was opposing the Motion, and we had to be on good form. I particularly recall that one of those inmates present (not one of those speaking) became so angry at some of the points made that he had to be taken back to his cell lest violence should break out. For several reasons, it was an evening to remember!

Talking of prisons, it was about that time that my ex-colleagues from Cheltenham Speakers Club were setting up the Leyhill Open Prison Speakers Club. Meetings were held both inside and outside the prison. Although it only lasted for three or four years, it did enable its members to develop a certain amount of speaking skill which hopefully was useful to them on their release.

Another highlight of my time in Croydon Speakers Club was even less expected. This one occurred at the end of a normal club meeting in the Blacksmith Arms. There were still 5 or 6 of us around, talking, when a stranger came into the room and talked to us. Unbelievably this was none other than the internationally famous illusionist, Uri Geller! He had stopped at the pub en route to his home in Berkshire, saw the notice saying that a speakers club was upstairs, and popped in to find out what it was all about. We explained about the club and, in the course of the discussion, he asked if anyone had a spoon. I went to the kitchen which was on that first floor and took out two spoons from a drawer. Uri took one from me, held it, stroked it, and – to our complete amazement – we saw it bend! It was not an illusion, and was certainly an entirely unexpected occasion which I for one shall never forget.

During these first two or three years in London, I was fairly reluctant to become too involved in Area activities. This was because I was unwilling to stay in London for the weekends, when club dinners and various meetings sometimes took place, but sought always to go back home to the family on the Friday evening. However I certainly kept up my attendances at the National Conference. These were always occasions to remember. The AGM and the seminars. The excellent skills of the speech and evaluation contestants. The Saturday evening gala dinner. There was too the cementing of the many friendships which I had already made – such as seeing Bill Mitchell, who had stayed at our Cheltenham house, becoming National President – seeing Peter Sterry, who had taken over from me in the Midlands, becoming National Development Officer – and seeing Ken Lewison become the first ASC member to receive the newly-created Advanced Certificate.

Friday evenings at Conference were an especial source of delight. Such events as the Millionaire's Evening in Telford and especially the Malt Whisky Trail at Perth come happily to mind. Then, once many had retired to bed late in the evening, what was once described as the "Fringe Festival" would commence. This tended to take the form of music provided especially by John McWhirter on guitar and Bill Mitchell on piano accordeon, with considerable hilarity and the ever-amusing Euan Anderson as the background. These were evenings to remember, even though the Saturday morning which followed might at times show the effect!

Back to normal club life, it was for the year 1990/1991 that I became President of Croydon Speakers Club. I recall that it was a largely uneventful year, in which the club and its members continued the steady progress of previous years. The Surrey Shield, for example, continued to be held and was, I believe, won by our own club. One meeting that I particularly remember during that year included an Evaluation Workshop conducted by Croydon club's first president, Jim Spinks. I found Jim's structure (brief talk/mini-speech/brief talk/speech/evaluation attempt(s)/final talk) an excellent way of training both new and existing members in what is quite possibly the most important element of a club evening. I am certainly not ashamed to say that I have used his exact Evaluation Workshop method myself quite a number of times since.

But perhaps the highlight of that year as Club President was the Annual Dinner which we held in a room in Croydon's renowned Fairfield Theatre. The reason is that it was our Anniversary Dinner, marking the 10th anniversary of Croydon Speakers Club, and all but one of the previous Presidents were able to attend. Having an Annual Dinner is a far less frequent feature of clubs in the south-east than it had been in the Midlands and certainly further north. However the 10th anniversary of this very successful speakers club clearly had to be celebrated with a Dinner, which was much enjoyed by all.

It was in that same year, 1990, that once again my personal life took an unexpected turn.

As had happened twice previously in my career in financial services marketing, the cause was a takeover and hence my own redundancy. On this occasion, I decided to bite the bullet and go into business on my own account. The route which I chose was to start a small market research company, specialising in qualitative research rather than questionnaire research, which I named Market Answers. As time went on, I added a syndicated research partnership – Corporate Answers – and a still very successful service company for the market research industry – Sample Answers.

One very early result of this, in 1991, was a membership survey for ASC.

There had always been questions related to the ASC and its members. For example, why did people join in the first place, why did some visitors fail to join, and why did some members leave? What was the demographic breakdown of people in speakers clubs? And what did they like or dislike about the club? Naturally there were opinions voiced about the answers to such questions, and these were sometimes conflicting. Now also some other issues were starting to emerge. It was Walter Hewson of Solihull who had written in The Speaker that "10,000 is the natural membership for ASC", and possibly this was still true. However the current figure was only a smallish proportion of this large figure. The statistics show a figure of 2698 for the year 1990, divided between 176 clubs. Moreover, another item in that same issue of The Speaker referred, to my great surprise, to the loss of 201 members in three years.

Research promised to provide some answers. I now had my own research company, and was able to provide research work – virtually for free – that would normally incur a fee of many hundreds of pounds, or even more.

The first step was to discuss the possibility of a survey with Peter Sterry, by now the National Development Officer, and gain his agreement. I then proceeded to devise a series of three self-completion questionnaires. The main one was for all current speakers club members, the second one was for a sample of those who had left the Association, and the third was for a sample of persons who had visited a club but had failed to join. The main questionnaire was inserted into all the Spring copies of The Speaker, which in those days was sent in bulk to every club for all their members. In addition, a mailing to clubs was used to help build the second and third samples. We then awaited the responses.

The volume of replies was by most market research standards quite exceptional. Almost 50% of ASC members spent the necessary 10 – 15 minutes to complete and return the full self-completion questionnaire, and good returns were also received from the samples of ex-members and non-joining visitors. The results were analysed, and a fully detailed 70 page report was prepared and made available at a nominal cost of £12 (to cover paper and printing). Many clubs took advantage of this. In addition some of the results were released in The Speaker, and a 12-page pamphlet of main results and implications to consider was mailed to every club.

The survey provided a wealth of information. Looking back many years later, certain key issues stand out. For example:

- What is the motivation for joining? For most it is first and foremost for speaking improvement and building confidence, especially for work reasons. Then, over time, liking for the club and the friendships made begin to be given as the main reasons for continuing as a member.

- Who are the members? At the time of the survey, 75% were over 45 and only 8% were under 35. The implications were obvious. It was fairly clear that, as a club grows in age, so does the age of its members tend to increase. This often makes recruiting – especially the highly important recruitment of younger persons – both necessary and more difficult.

- Why did some members leave and certain visitors fail to join? Many reasons were given, and clubs needed to assess their own rating on certain key problem areas. For example, did the club – or would the club – really meet the educational promise for which people joined? The world has changed greatly since the pre-Internet era of 1991, but many of the issues discovered probably still apply.

One unexpected eventuality for me was becoming District President. This was for the year 1992/1993. The reason, in a nutshell, was that the prospective District President, Keith Dickerson, had been called away to work in Brussels for a year or two. It was known that I had had the experience of District Vice-Presidency when I was in the Midlands District, and it was suggested that I should take the post of South Eastern District President for that year. Unexpected, but certainly an honour, and one which I was very pleased to accept.

I recall some of the headings on the framework plan which I drafted for myself in readiness. Words such as Admin. Education. Development (numbers and new clubs). Then a few more specific items. District publication? Area teams? 2-day AGM? Topics contest? Clubs in firms? Force of skilled trainers? Some of these would start to be tackled during my year of office. Others, regrettably, I never tackled. However one task which I did achieve was to introduce the annual award of an 'Ace of Clubs' Trophy for the best club in South Eastern District, chosen on the basis of the 4 criteria of numbers, standards, initiative (or initiatives) and ASC involvement.

One task was to get to know the whole of the District. South Eastern District's East Area had been largely unknown to me until then. I therefore tried to find time to visit clubs such as Chelmsford, Felixstowe, Ipswich, Brentwood and Bury St Edmunds. Colchester was a special case. By chance, several of its small band of members had temporarily moved away for work reasons. Meetings were going to be suspended for a year, but the Club would still like to retain its charter and resume meetings in a year or two's time. As District President, I was able to get NEC's agreement that a temporarily dormant club could continue in membership for a year or two on payment of one single capitation fee.

I also needed to find out more about the two or three London clubs north of the Thames, and those somewhat further afield both in Potters Bar where I was born (the Oakmere Speakers Club) and in Bletchley. Some were particularly enthusiastic. Oakmere's Jane Knight, for example, pushed hard for a Topics Contest to be included at all levels in the end-year contest programme. I am pleased to recall that this innovation actually took place, firstly at District level and secondly (in 1995, I believe) at National level. (An oddment of history is that the first National Topics Final was seen as an entertainment gimmick and had taken place at around midnight on the Friday of the 1994 National Conference. However the experiment was much liked, and the following year saw the introduction of the National Topics Contest – judged by the audience as a whole – as a proper third contest for the Association).

As District President, I served that year as a member of NEC. The National President was Ron Robb, and I recall it as being both an enjoyable and productive flow of meetings. One particular initiative in the year concerned speaking courses. The value of such courses, whether to meet the educational objectives or the recruitment objectives of ASC, had become obvious both to NEC's Education Committee and to its Development Committee. It was therefore decided to carry out a National Speaking Course Campaign.

Responsibility for the task was given to Midlander Geoff Ashton (whose canal boat was the venue for some of our meetings) and myself. The way we did it was to put together a mailing package that would be sent to every club. The front page consisted of 'testimonials' for three very successful course initiatives. These were the London Insurance Institute course, the 'Effective Speaking' pre-meeting 6-session course from Cheltenham and Croydon, and the course developed by Ken Sharpe in Stockport. The interior of the mailing package consisted of examples and further advice on what could be done, and the club mailing duly took place.

Being a member of NEC (i.e. National Executive Committee) at that time also brought me much closer to an important recent initiative – the Speaker of the Year award. The original concept was born in discussion between Peter Sterry and Chris Birch in Development Committee, which Peter Sterry was running at that time as ASC's National Development Officer. Every year ASC should decide on and appoint a well-known person as Speaker of the Year. The publicity potential was evident, though how to choose the recipient was less evident. Indeed many different methods were adopted as the years rolled on.

It was decided that the award would be a commemoration bowl of Caithness Glass, and the first Speaker of the Year was chosen. This was Peter Ustinov, and the year was 1989. Peter Ustinov accepted, and the trophy was presented to him by ASC's current and immediate past National Presidents, Drummond Hutchinson and Hugh McKenzie, at Aberdeen Airport between two flights that Peter Ustinov was making.

Some reservations were voiced about the following year's choice, who was Edwina Currie MP. She was certainly a very good and lively speaker. However she was currently much in the news primarily due to a mistaken statement she had made that most chickens in this country were suffering from salmonella. In fact she turned out to be an excellent choice, making quite a number of visits to speakers clubs within the Midlands, nearer to where she lived. As to the question of publicity value of the award, which has been at times queried, I remember mentioning this Award as an extra item of interest in our club's normal speakers club press releases, and I enclosed a photograph of Edwina Currie. The release was published by two newspapers, and in both cases the photograph also appeared. The Speaker of the Year story could give publicity, but it was up to the clubs to do the work.

The story does not end there, by the way. Although there was as yet no formal Speaker of the Year Dinner, a year and a half later Edwina Currie herself invited the Association to hold a dinner in the Houses of Parliament, for which she was the formal host. By that time I was the incoming District President, and the event turned out to be a most pleasant occasion for me personally. The reason was that, while the 100+ attendees took their guided tours around the House of Commons and House of Lords, I spent a happy hour on the Terrace in the company of Edwina, and still owe her for the two drinks she bought me that evening. (I better explain that, as a visitor to Parliament, I was not allowed to buy the drinks myself!)

The tradition of holding a special Dinner for the Speaker of the Year Award was begun by South Western District's John Grigg for ASC's third Speaker of the Year in 1991. This was for John Harvey Jones, the ex-MD of ICI and well known to TV audiences as a remarkable business guru from his 'Troubleshooter' programmes. The venue chosen was the Hatherley Manor Court Hotel just outside Gloucester and the event was a superb success. Clearly the Speaker of the Year himself was delighted to receive the award, and all of us who were present were treated to an excellent acceptance speech.

I was especially pleased to have experienced that dinner since I myself inherited most of the responsibility for arranging the following year's event. It was seven years since Terry Waite, the envoy of the Archbishop of Canterbury, had been kidnapped in Beirut and held as a prisoner. He was then released from captivity and was flown back to the UK. His speech on leaving the plane at Lyneham airport was broadcast all over the country and made an immediate impact. Most specifically, it led to the invitation to become the ASC Speaker of the Year for 1992, which he was pleased to accept. The Dinner held for him at the Cafe Royal in October 1992 proved memorable in every way. I served as MC for that festive occasion, and was particularly pleased that my choice of supporting speaker, responding to the Toast to the Guests, was able to be Michael Morris MP, chairman of Ways and Means, who had been a business colleague a few years before he had entered Parliament. I was also pleased that the Vote of Thanks was given by my colleague from Cheltenham in those pre-mixed club days of 10 years previously, Pam Sewell. Incidentally my own links with Terry Waite have continued on several occasions since that time, though not in connection with ASC.

Yet there is one memory of my year as District President in 1992/1993 which really stands out even more strikingly. That was the visit to South Eastern District by members of the Moscow Speakers Club. This certainly must be counted as an important event in the whole history of ASC.

The story really started the year before, in 1991. It was the time of Gorbachev's glasnost initiative, and the opening of Russia to the Western world. One of the unofficial business ambassadors working in Moscow at that time was Bill Finley, who was a senior member of Leeds Speakers Club. He discovered that very few Muscovites were willing or able to give a speech, and certainly not in public. They had after all been prohibited from doing this for over 60 years. But now, to take part in the modern world, communication skills had become necessary. The answer, he quickly realised, could be a speakers club. He therefore spent time interesting those about him, and briefing them on the workings of the speakers clubs here in Britain. This clearly rang a bell, and the interest even extended as far as some Russians translating ASC's own speakers guide. The first meeting of the Moscow Speakers Club actually took place in 1992, and its membership quickly grew to over 100.

It was Ken Richardson of Croydon Speakers Club who, in consultation with Bill Finley, thought up a plan for members of the Moscow Speakers Club to come and stay with our own speakers club members in the London area. This was not a question of ordinary tourism. The rouble income of Moscow residents at that time, in international financial terms, was worth only a tiny amount in British pounds, thus the British hosts would have to pay for everything. However the plan worked and about 20 Moscow speakers club members came over and stayed for 2 weeks in the homes of various South Eastern District club members.

The first event of their stay was to visit the Houses of Parliament and to be welcomed by our earlier Speaker of the Year, Edwina Currie. I myself was particularly fortunate since the Russian visit coincided with my own year as District President. Thus as well as inviting Russians to our own Croydon club meeting (and hence evaluating a speech in a language that I did not understand – try this at some time!), I was able to invite the 20 Russians plus their hosts to the District Conference which I decided to hold that year in Cambridge.

The District Council agreed to hold an Eve-of-Conference dinner in Cambridge, and some of the Russians attended. The 'fun' element was a balloon debate. I am pleased to say that our guests played their full part, with three Russians taking the roles of Mrs Gorbachev, Yuri Gagarin and Mr Kalashnikov respectively. The following day, which was the day of our District Conference, was a further memorable occasion. Whilst some of us carried out the business of the AGM in the morning, the Russian visitors plus their hosts enjoyed a tour of Cambridge. They then came to our meeting in the afternoon, to receive a welcome by the Mayor of Cambridge and to enjoy the various speech contests.

I think that it was the following year that there was further close communication with the members of the Moscow Speakers Club. This centred on Ken Sharpe and others in the Stockport area who arranged for some ASC members to visit Moscow. I was not involved, but believe that everything went very well. Sadly, however, I have heard nothing about the Moscow Speakers Club nor activity anywhere else in Russia since those days.

As readers will probably have gathered, I had very much enjoyed my District President year of 1992/1993. But all good things come to an end, and it was finally time to return back to a more normal speakers club life.

In 1984, Wolverhampton Speakers Club held their 25th Anniversary dinner in the Members' Dining Room of the House of Commons, where the club's immediate past president, Roger King, was now an MP. Those shown are, from the left: Len Mears (then National President), Roger King MP, Fred Higgins (Club President) and Barry Picken (Midlands District President).

ASC's first female National President, Hilary Hampshaw, making a presentation to long-serving officer Ken Grubb of Cheltenham Speakers Club.

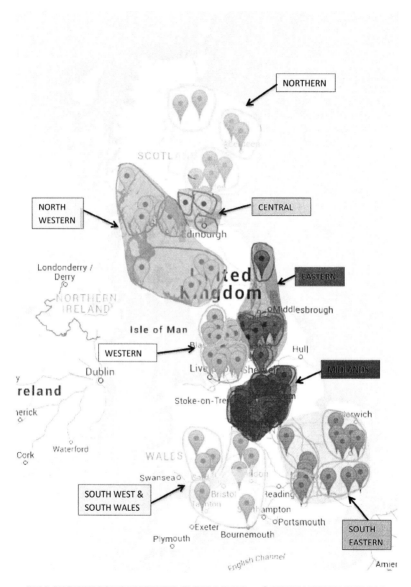

MAP SHOWING THE DISTRICTS, THEIR AREAS and CLUBS WITHIN THE ASC

Ken Lewison is shown receiving the first Advanced Certificate of Achievement from National President, Hugh McKenzie.

The 'Melody Twins', Bill Mitchell (squeezebox) and John McWhirter (guitar), entertaining us with their late Friday night 'Fringe Festival' at the Annual Conference back in the 80s.

The first recipient of the Association's Speaker of the Year Award was the stage, film and BBC performer Peter Ustinov. He is seen receiving the Award – a Caithness Glass Goblet – from National President Drummond Hutchison (on the right) together with Immediate Past President Hugh McKenzie.

Some of the recipients of ASC's annual Speaker of the Year award. From left to right: Lord (Digby) Jones, Edwina Currie MP, Simon Weston, Terry Waite, Esther Rantzen.

Chapter 4

One Millennium comes to an end. . . . . .

Over time I had become a much more frequent attendee at Horsham Speakers Club. One reason for this was to assist its founder, Jim Johnston. Jim was an exceptional person in his energy and vision but, unfortunately, had to endure a very difficult stammer. Those people who come along to a speakers club for the first time naturally look for more fluent speakers to seek to emulate. At Horsham, I and one or two others needed to fill that role. My contributions included the occasional tutorial or evaluation workshop and in 1992 I joined the club. A year later, I – together with Ken Richardson and Jim's early helper Lois Broadhurst – received from Jim a Certificate of Honorary Membership. (Despite this, I can assure my fellow members that I have continued ever since to pay my full fees to the club!)

Just one more step was required. The club now had the necessary 12 members but still needed to receive its official ASC charter. In April 1993, Jim came with me to the ASC National Conference, held that year in Bristol, and received the club's Charter from the hands of the National President, John Grigg. It was a proud moment for Jim. Also, from then on, I counted Horsham Speakers Club as my principal club and, in fact, ceased my Croydon membership just one or two years later.

Following my year as District President, I agreed to take on the role of South Eastern District Treasurer/Secretary, and continued in this role for some four or five years. It was a period when the District was running smoothly. Volunteers were coming forward to take office without undue pressure. Indeed I recall a report written during that period which said "The area is blessed with a plethora of willing and capable persons."

For instance, it was fairly normal for a District seminar to be held during the year. One that I particularly recall was on the theme of "Strengthening the club". Another event stands out in my mind because it was held in the prestigious venue of the Post Office Tower, thanks to the influence of BT executive Keith Dickerson who, after just two or three years in Brussels, had returned to this country.

As far as my own District Treasurer role was concerned, we encouraged each Area to hold one special event per year which District would help fund, and wrote this into the District budget. Also, to help make sure that every club paid its dues to District and to National on time, we developed a policy of asking the club to send a single cheque, covering both these charges, to District. We at District then forwarded the national capitation element onto the National Treasurer. This certainly ensured that all clubs paid both National and District on time and that records were full and accurate, though the system occasionally had to be argued through with NEC.

On the negative side, what unfortunately started to become clear was that, despite ASC's tremendous sales story, growth could no longer be taken for granted. For example, new clubs were becoming more of a rarity even in the south-east, despite the many lessons that had been learnt on method and motivation.

Naturally there were attempts to take corrective action. At national level, for instance, ASC advertised in The Speaker for a Publicity Officer who would be additional to the National Development Officer. I am not sure if this post was ever filled. One new method tried by the Association was to have an ASC stand in the Institute for Personal Development's annual conference and exhibition held in Harrogate in, I believe, 1995. In South Eastern District, we monitored closely the leads which sprang from this initiative, and found the method useful. I never discovered the results in other Districts, and having a stand in that exhibition was not repeated.

ASC has often been described as "the best kept secret". To help solve this publicity problem, I personally spent some time exploring the possibility of converting ASC's in-house magazine 'The Speaker' into, say, a 20-page magazine that might be called Effective Speaking Quarterly and would cover the wider field of spoken communication. To be produced in association with ASC, it would be sold to the public through WHSmith and other outlets. The idea was that ASC members should still receive the magazine free, and that their copies should contain, say, an 8-page insert of ASC news. I discussed this concept with my erstwhile Cheltenham friend Heming Branum who, by this time, was National Development Officer. Unfortunately we were defeated by commercial cost factors and took this type of step no further.

Until later on in the 90s, ASC had no active competitors, so survival was not at all an issue. But growth <u>was</u> an issue and, if ASC were to achieve its potential, then further thinking of some sort was clearly implied. I shall be talking about this in the next chapter, but meanwhile return to Horsham Speakers Club.

My own time was spent mainly on club life. Now that the club which he had started was chartered and firmly grounded, Jim Johnson retired from the presidency, and new single-year Presidents such as Norma Elston and Brian Fry began to be elected. Under their excellent leadership, the club programme continued in its positive way. Outside Horsham, there would occasionally be meetings with other ASC speakers clubs such as North Surrey and the new Weald Speakers Club at Tunbridge Wells. We created our own team contest, the Sussex Pride, mainly for competition against ASC's Brighton Speakers Club. Within Horsham, events such as a 'tall story' contest or an Any Questions session might start to appear in the programme. I recall for example a debate on living in Horsham versus living in London, and the occasional outside speaker, such as one who gave us an insightful talk on 'The Samaritans'.

One of my own activities in Horsham Speakers Club during those middle years of the 90s was to run a standard pre-meeting 5- or 6-session Effective Speaking course each autumn. This certainly helped to ensure a good flow members (and to provide a small financial benefit) to the club, as well as enabling the speakers club to feel that it was offering a good service to the people of Horsham.

Indeed Horsham Speakers Club became very much part of the town's life. This included having a good working relationship with the town's largest employer, Royal & Sun Alliance, who twice allowed us to host an exhibition in their foyer entitled "10 Steps to Speaking Effectiveness". On one occasion, I myself was asked to give some minutes of coaching to the company's debating team which was going to take part in an industry event. I also recall being on another occasion the MC at the annual dinner of the Insurance Institute of Horsham and Crawley. Indeed, looking back I find it not at all surprising that I even started to consider moving from London (where I now lived full-time) down to this delightful market town.

There was another and much more unexpected reason also for feeling a part of Horsham life. This began one evening in November 1993. Jim asked me if I would stay behind after the club meeting and have a drink as there was something he wished to talk about. I naturally agreed. We adjourned to the Old Kings Head's bar and Jim showed me a leaflet about an arts festival in Dorset, and a poster about another which was due to take place somewhere in Hampshire. I looked at them and waited for him to speak. His next words were "I think we should have an arts festival in Horsham". "Yes", I agreed, "That could be interesting." The story went on. Jim was thinking about holding an open meeting in the town about it. Pause. In fact he had already fixed an open meeting for a week's time. Pause. More than that, he had invited the director of the Horsham Arts Centre (later 'The Capitol') and a senior master (and poet) from the nearby Christ's Hospital 'Bluecoat' School to talk at that meeting. Pause. It simply needed a chairman to run the meeting, so would I agree to be that chairman?

I have always found it difficult to say "No" and this time was no exception. I therefore found myself a week later chairing a meeting of leading arts, community and council figures from the Horsham area in the District Council's own premises. Everything went well, there was enthusiasm for the project, ideas were forthcoming, and it was decided to move to the next stage.

Thus it was that a couple of days later I was in contact with nearby resident Sir Michael Checkland, who had quite recently resigned as Director-General of the BBC, to discover if he was prepared to become Chairman of the West Sussex Arts Festival. His answer was positive and he proved to be a highly capable and completely hands-on Chairman. And so, for the next dozen years, 'Arts Fanfare'– as it became named – was to prove a large and hugely enjoyable feature in Horsham and West Sussex life.

Arts Fanfare covered a wide spread of arts, and included both professional and amateur performances. I took on the role of Secretary of the festival whilst Jim initially organised the literature programme. After two or three years, he found it difficult to continue, so I took over the literature side also.

This book is not the place to write the history of Arts Fanfare. Suffice it to say my share of the organising, which included putting on seven or eight literary events for each Arts Fanfare until 2004, was both demanding and enjoyable. My activity not only included arranging and frequently chairing a wide spread of debates, lectures, and school and other literary contests, but also involved working very closely with presenters ranging from the ex-KGB Russian spy Oleg Gordievsky to home-grown talents such as Colin Dexter, Terry Waite (again!) and Benjamin Zephaniah.

Back to speakers club life, it was in the spring of 1996 that two new visitors came to one of our regular speakers club meetings. Their names were Richard Kilroy and Lesley Dunn. Like all (or certainly most) of the club's visitors, Richard and Lesley were reasonably impressed. But unlike most, they were sufficiently impressed to ask if we at Horsham Speakers Club would help them set up a speakers club in Redhill where they had their offices. Three months later, with Richard as President, Redhill & Reigate speakers club held its opening meeting. By the end of August 1996, there had been 4 meetings which had included 7 icebreakers. By the end of the 1996/1997 season, the club had 17 members and, of course, had chartered.

At the start of its life, the club met in a conference room within Richard's company's offices. From there, we were fortunate to be able to soon move to the premises of the Constitutional Club, which had bar facilities. I was a founding member of the club, and remain a full member to the present day. Also joining and giving good help in those early days were regular speakers such as Fergal Hogan, previously from West Kent club, and lay reader David Whitmore from Oxted, both of whom I shall mention again in later pages. Meanwhile let me move on from talking about my own two clubs to the national scene at that time.

My mention of Terry Waite three or four paragraphs ago brings me back to ASC's annual Speaker of the Year dinners which continued to be very popular events and were held in various locations. All of us who attended were both honoured and highly entertained by being able to listen to radio and television personalities such as Kate Adie and James Naughtie, and to leading political figures such as Tony Benn and the then Speaker of the House of Commons (and now Dame) Betty Boothroyd. All were memorable occasions, but two in particular stand out for me.

The first was the Speaker of the Year Dinner for the Glasgow Herald columnist Jack Webster – or, as many south of the border referred to him – 'Jack who'? Partly I recall the event because of our speaker's cordial personality and the content of his speech that evening. He described, for example, the Clydeside design and construction of the liner Queen Mary, particularly mentioning the part played by shipbuilder heir John Brown – and to all our amazement, John Brown was actually present that evening! But I also recall that dinner because Jack Webster had actually suffered from a stammer in his early days, and had successfully overcome it, finally to achieve the accolade of Speaker of the Year. It was an emotional story for him and for all of us.

I also vividly remember the Victoria Wood dinner, which was very well organised by Horsham member Norma Elston. This was not only due to our Speaker of the Year's excellent "comedy routine" (rather than a speech!) which she delivered to us all on that occasion. It was also because Sir Michael Checkland, who was by then a warm friend, agreed to give the response to the Toast to the Guests. In addition I had brought with me as my personal guest that evening someone else with a strong BBC background. This was a fairly recent friend Barbara Braden, whom I had got to know quite well in a different connection. She was better known in her maiden name Barbara Kelly when she achieved broadcasting fame in the programme 'What's my Line?' back in the 50s and 60s.

The Speaker of the Year Dinner was, of course, one of the two big annual ASC events. The other was National Conference. The opportunity to enjoy the friendship and activities of the annual national conference is one of the great privileges offered by the ASC, as had been shown clearly by the results of the 1991 survey. One member in fact likened attendance as "Going up for the Cup". One of my own main memories of those years of the mid-90s is being asked to give a speech at his inaugural dinner in 1994 by incoming National

President, Murdo Morrison, which was certainly a great honour. But National Conference was to play an even greater part of my ASC speaking journey in April 1999.

During those years of the 90s, Peter Sterry and I, together with Scotsman Bob Campbell, had been the members of the informal Conference Action Group, set up originally by a previous National President, Eric Taylor, which assisted ASC in national conference matters. My own chief contribution had been to bring the "Conference Guide" manual fully up-to-date, which was one of the CAG's responsibilities. Another main responsibility was to oversee the location for the conference each year. South Eastern District was chosen for the 1998/1999 annual conference, a Watford venue was suggested by the Conference Search consultant team who were being used at that time – and was agreed – and I was chosen by the District to be Conference Convenor. This role required my attendance at the 1998/1999 NEC meetings. More importantly, such an undertaking required a great amount of planning and a full conference planning team. One of the many benefits of ASC membership is that it can at times greatly help the development of teamwork ability

It was a busy year and a half. There was of course the initial need to benefit from the experience of the previous year's conference convenor (thank you Mary Smith of Solihull!) and also to maintain full communication via The Speaker magazine with clubs and individuals all over the country. Additionally, within South Eastern District, we created and issued our own quarterly District Newsletter during the year leading up to the conference. A particularly important role in conference planning was that of the chief steward, one of whose key tasks was to maintain close contact with National Education Officer Lilian Watts to ensure that the all-important annual contests ran smoothly. I was fortunate in having Trevor Havelock in that role, whilst Norma Elston who had been a successful Speaker of the Year dinner organiser, took on the role of Treasurer.

Conference is not only a time for the serious matters of an annual general meeting, contest finals and educational and development seminars. It is also a time to have fun and enjoy oneself. This proved to be the case at Watford. For our Friday evening extravaganza, our own National Speech Contest winner from 1997, May Park – almost a Cockney herself – chaired a Cockney

Evening of music and laughter, complete with Pearly Queen. Hatfield House was the venue for a successful Saturday afternoon Partners' Outing. Then, in the evening, we were delighted to enjoy the presence of the Mayor of Watford who turned out to be a charming and very lively lady in her 30s. One of the abiding memories of the Watford conference was the fact that, not only had she accepted an invitation to the Gala Dinner, but that she was still leading the post-dinner dancing until 1 AM or 2 AM, much to the delight of all present, particularly those attending from Scotland.

The Watford AGM was also the scene for one of the most important technological advances of the ASC. As mentioned earlier, one member of the recently-formed Redhill & Reigate club was Fergal Hogan who now lived in a delightful village near (far too near!) the Gatwick Airport flight path. His help for the new club had included running a particularly successful seminar on speaking development, but his day job was holding a senior position in IT development.

As The Speaker of the time had pointed out in an article, although a few members such as the south-east's Dennis Carlyle were starting to use the recently developed practice of email on a personal level, the ASC as a whole had only the most rudimentary web arrangements. This fact was also briefly remarked on in the course of an NEC meeting which I attended, though no action was agreed. Back in Redhill, however, IT enthusiast Fergal was stressing to us the importance of the IT advances. This was clearly a matter for major action, and it was apparent to me that Fergal was the person to start it.

The result of my discussions with Fergal was that he proposed a Motion for the General Council meeting at Watford, urging the need for a definite ASC website, ASC Webmaster, and ASC web address (viz www.the-ASC.org.uk), and proposing the setting up of a working group to implement the arrangements. This Motion was duly passed at conference, and the rest is history. Fergal's working party was set up and in due course provided its report to the NEC. Shortly after this, Fergal unfortunately had to give up the Webmaster position for business reasons, but Lilian Watts, on the conclusion of her term as ASC's Education Officer, took over that position and development proceeded apace.

As I look back, my speaking journey both in the two clubs of which I was a member and in the national events which I attended was continuing happily in those final years of the 2nd Millennium AD. The Watford conference too had been a success, and South Eastern District had by no means let ASC and its members down. Some of us had started to feel real concern about the future of ASC, but I'll leave that until the next chapter. However there is just one further item which I should mention in this chapter before we pass on to the new millennium.

This was a letter which I received in December 1994 from a person previously unknown to me, whose name was Magnus Nielsen. He wrote: "I am the Secretary of the Cogers Society, a group meeting on Saturday evenings in the Betsey Trotwood pub in Clerkenwell. We are the last surviving "Coffee House Debating Society", an authentic tradition dating back to the 18th century", and so on. I duly acknowledged the letter and expressed my potential interest, though apologising that I could not attend on Saturday evenings as I was away from London every weekend. It was two or three years later that I next heard about it. This was the announcement that Magnus Nielsen would be running a Cogers Demonstration Debate at the Insurance Institute Speakers Club on the club's regular evening.

The reason that I mention this is that, for me personally, it can only be described as a life-affecting incident. I attended that meeting, and the whole field of debating and also some additional organisations became added to my 'speaking journey' from that time. But these non-ASC parts of the journey I shall leave to the final chapter and meanwhile continue, in Chapter 5, with my ASC part of that journey.

Chapter 5

. . . . . . and a new Millennium begins

Following the intensity of my 'Conference Convenor' year, my speakers club life returned to its normal pattern.

For the wider world, those few months leading up to the arrival of a new millennium were the time of the millennium bug – the problem expected by many to cause worldwide damage to the Internet, but which proved to have been a false alarm. For ASC, 1999/2000 was the very successful year of our first female National President, Hilary Hampshaw, whose husband Colin had been National President some 20 years before. But before I start telling my own speaking story for those first years of the new millennium, I need to go back to 1997.

ASC's situation, as I've already described, was that the south-east – along with the south-west – was a part of the country where speakers clubs were thin on the ground. If the south-east had possessed the same 'clubs-per-head ratio as in Scotland, we would have nearer to 200 clubs than 20. The need was just as great. But despite the logic, and despite our own wishes and exhortations, the club gaps were not being filled and visitors were not flooding into the clubs which existed. Clearly something was missing.

It was against this background that several of us who were interested in furthering the development of ASC started to meet and discuss the issue, first informally but then in a more structured way. As well as me, our core group consisted of Julie McLeod of Fairfield club (who was soon to become Area President), Neville White of Insurance Institute club, and Bob Wise of Croydon club who, a year or two earlier, had been District President. Others such as Fergal Hogan and Horsham's David Weaver also joined us at times.

We agreed on the problem. Against the odds, ASC growth was not happening. Indeed there was evidence that some clubs in various parts of the country were declining, or even closing.

There was also reluctant agreement that the current way in which the ASC was hoping for growth – at the top end through the NEC's development structure: at the bottom end by the efforts and interest of individual clubs – was proving not to be the answer. National Development Officers and also their yearly-changing committees had always tended to see their role mainly as sales support, especially for existing clubs, rather than as marketing strategy – and the two are leagues apart. Individual clubs were more concerned with their own internal numbers than with evangelising to the world outside.

A further element was that, after 25 years of apparent dormancy, there was starting to be a marked rise in Toastmasters club activity within the south-east.

It was the work aspect that seemed to be key. The evidence showed that the reason why most ASC members had joined was to increase their skills and confidence, especially in their work situation, yet we were clearly missing out badly on attracting those in early career or even mid-career. Employers large and small, both private and public sector, could be our best ambassadors, and it would be in their interest as well as in that of their employees. However there was not a single piece of ASC support literature nor any business presentation aimed at HR departments. This lack of focus had to be rectified. How best to do it?

These discussions were leading on to considering structure. ASC consisted of a large number of autonomous clubs. There was no disagreement with that composition. Indeed the whole point of our conversations was to help these autonomous clubs grow and prosper. But was the overall structure the best vehicle for growth? Should there perhaps be something different from the current structure which was more able to achieve growth (and thus help the clubs)? Maybe South Eastern District could show the way ahead.

As an example, going back in time, we noted when ASC left Toastmasters, and also later on at the suggestion of a previous National President, Bill Mitchell, there had been discussion about the formation of an Institute of

Public Speaking. Such a body would have the useful hallmark of 'authority' and possibly give 'accreditations'. However the purpose of an Institute was more for education purposes than for growth purposes, and thus it was not quite what we were looking for. In any case 'Institute' was a protected word that was unlikely to be permitted legally for ASC use, especially now that a public speaking competitor was starting to emerge.

Discussions moved on to a more sales-y approach – some kind of body that would stress the importance, help the finance, provide some training, and also encourage the firm's employees to join the local speakers club. We envisaged its being based initially in the south-east but quickly moving northwards. The precise link with ASC – some form of integrated management at one end: separate bodies at the other end – would need much more discussion.

At this stage we decided to talk through the emerging concepts, on a confidential basis, with six or seven leading South Eastern District members, each of whom had had NEC experience. Their replies proved to be broadly positive. Our analysis and our suggested focus and solution made good sense and should potentially succeed. But yes, the link with ASC would need more discussion, and especially sensitive handling.

Regrettably at this point the group disbanded. The reason was one of time and commitment. One of our core group was starting a new job, another was starting her own new company and a third was moving away. In any case, concentrating on planning for Watford was a greater priority. Sad to say, we never reassembled, and the matter was left unfinished. It took four or five years before discussions were to start again.

Leaving aside these deeper issues, I recall that South Eastern District was seeing some excellent growth initiatives at around that time. As mentioned earlier, Wimbledon Speakers Club had suddenly arrived on the scene with much impact, thanks to the drive of Debra Owen-Hughes. Fairfield Speakers Club did well under the leadership of Julie McLeod, and then became even more go-ahead as it transformed itself into Speakers of Bromley and went on to found Beckenham Speakers Club. Slightly further afield Trevor Havelock started a speakers club at Reading, whilst Trevor Kenning founded one at Ashford in Kent, though regrettably neither club lasted too long. There were other initiatives too. For example, a Bexhill club was started and ran for a few months, whilst Horsham briefly explored the possibility of a club in Worthing, largely to replace the Brighton Speakers Club which had unfortunately withdrawn from the Association.

I continued as a member both of the Horsham and the Redhill & Reigate clubs. Horsham Speakers Club was particularly buoyant during those years. Sadly our founder, Jim Johnston, passed away, but several members made a big impact. Let me mention some of them.

Librarian Paul Cheeseman had joined the club in the mid-90s, gave a memorable first speech about his travels in Tashkent, and rapidly advanced to run the club's autumn 6-session pre-meeting course for three or four years. By the turn of the millennium, he had become District Secretary, and it was a loss to both the club and the Association when a new job and a new wife took him away to Canada for more than 10 years. The good news is that he and his wife have now returned to the UK.

Des Downey also joined at that time, and rose to become Club President in his 80th year. On his actual birthday, the club had arranged a surprise "This is your Life" evening for Des. He had been a 'desert rat' in the 8th Army in the war, and had also once started a dance band. Much more recently he was the founder of "Horsham in Bloom", which had won the South of Britain trophy. A stimulating event in the club around that time was a formal debate of the Motion "that gardening should be banned in Horsham", proposed by Paul Cheeseman and - not unexpectedly – passionately opposed by Des.

Richard Mosley won the National Evaluation Contest at the 2001 ASC conference in Nairn. He is still Horsham Speakers Club's only national winner. I remember two highly useful evaluation workshop evenings which he ran in the club, both of them illustrated by four speakers. In one of these, the speeches given were at Levels 1 to 4, whilst in the other the speeches given were at Levels 5 to 8.

David Weaver, as Club President, started the practice of sending a lively and informative letter to members and potential members after every club meeting. This practice has continued and is undoubtedly one of the reasons why Horsham meetings normally have an attendance of around 20 persons. David also led a trip by Horsham club members across the water to a highly enjoyable joint meeting with a Dublin Toastmasters club in St Patrick's week, while he was President. This was certainly a unique event for a Sussex-based ASC club!

Finally let me mention Tony Hull, who was a local councillor as well as a member of Horsham Speakers Club. In conjunction with David Weaver and the club's treasurer, Tony obtained a £2452 lottery grant for the club in 2006, thus providing us with video and other superb equipment. (Unsurprisingly, on hearing this, one or two other clubs followed Horsham's example and also benefited from lottery grants). Also thanks to Tony, we and nearby clubs had the opportunity of a superb voice projection and topics evening in Horsham's modern and palatial council chamber.

My other speakers club, Redhill & Reigate, was also well-attended and lively during that period. Its founder, Richard Kilroy, moved on after those all-important early years, but donated to the club the Kilroy Trophy for presentation to someone at every meeting. My own main role for some years was to run our standard pre-meeting course once a year, which maintained the satisfactory numbers. An annual dinner was introduced to the club's programme, and proved popular.

Members such as Lindsay Cole stand out. I shall always remember Lindsay's presentation of "The Noscars" trophies at our dinner in his presidential year. For example:

Category for award:
    Quality of the meeting chairman's opening comments:

Nominations:
    Paul – "Good evening ladies and gentlemen, and welcome to Redhill and Reigate speakers club"
    Mary –"Good evening ladies and gentlemen, and welcome to what I'm sure will be a very enjoyable meeting"
    Jenny – "Good evening ladies and gentlemen, and I'm delighted to see so many people here for what will be a busy evening of speaking"

Andy – "Hey Fergal, is this your beer?"

Winner of the NOSCAR for Chairman's opening comments
Andy

.... and one additional NOSCAR award, this one being for "Most Memorable Sentence from a speech", went to Ted Aston whose speech entitled "Amateur radio broadcasting made simple" had included the Memorable Sentence "If you've got good equipment, frequency is not a problem".

Thanks to the advent of IT, some of our routines were changing. I remember asking the National Secretary of the time, Diana Dickinson, "Email is fast becoming the norm for many people. Could clubs have the option of receiving national communication by email rather than through the post?" (A couple of years later, Diana herself wrote in her annual report, that 'In contrast to when I first took office four years ago, the majority now of my daily tasks is answering emails. Fewer ASC phone calls are made; fewer letters are posted".)

For me, it was a relaxed period of my ASC life. One task which came my way was being asked by National Education Director Terry Kinsman to draft a revised Manual section on "Gestures and Body Language", which I was pleased to do. I was also invited to attend and speak at Cheltenham club's 21st anniversary dinner. This for me was of course a very special occasion. Another memorable occasion was Maidstone's Annual Dinner in the same year as the Watford Conference, which had Ann Widdecombe as its special guest. I also much enjoyed the national conferences and the Speaker of the Year annual dinners which took place in those years. These included the only Speaker of the Year Luncheon which ever took place. Receiving the award that year was Patricia Routledge, known to the whole nation as the social climber Mrs Bouquet and certainly not as Mrs Bucket.

But then another unexpected eventuality occurred which led to my agreeing to become President of South Eastern District in 2001/2002.

The background was a long-standing issue of Area structure. The South East Area of South Eastern District had for several years contained about 10 clubs, stretching from the Isle of Thanet right across to Kingston-on-Thames, and including clubs such as Horsham and Brighton in Sussex. There was no larger Area in the whole of ASC. After all, most Areas consisted of just 4 or 5 clubs. In 1990, South Eastern member Dennis Ogden wrote a letter suggesting that the South East Area should be split. An area of this size, he said, was almost unmanageable, both for reasons of travel mileage and also since it was difficult to be in close enough contact with each club. Another senior South Easterner, Terry Kinsman, responded. The Area's large size, he wrote, gave it strength, including a prestigious end-year contest and general meeting.

No action was taken at this time. However some five or six years later, a compromise solution (or, as some considered it, a "fudge") had been introduced. This was to have both an 'East' and a 'West' Area Vice-President, and also to split the yearly contest meeting into two meetings. But in 2000/2001 the issue came up again in a meeting of South Eastern District Council, a vote was taken, and the decision was made to completely split this large Area into two smaller Areas, named respectively South Area and Kent Area.

Unfortunately this led to considerable acrimony between two or three individuals, and finally to some resignations from office. In particular, a new District President would need to be found for the year 2001/2002. Not being linked in any way with either side of the dispute, I was asked if I would be prepared to stand in as South Eastern District President, to which I agreed. Unexpected, but certainly once again a great honour.

Feelings had reached a high level during the dispute. My immediate task as the new District President was to ensure that we had a period of calm. This, I believe, was achieved. The two new Area Presidents, for South Area and for Kent Area respectively, soon bedded themselves down, and speakers club life continued in both parts of what had been a short time before just one single South East Area.

I remember my District Presidency as being a full and busy year. My own clubs were doing well, and there were visits to be made to other clubs. Team-speaking as well as a seminar in most years was a feature of South Eastern District. In fact, only a few years later, no less than seven teams competed on the theme "Money is happiness" in the team-speaking contest.

Highlight of the District year, however, continued to be the District's annual general and contest meeting. Suspense always lasted right to the end. Who would be the winners of the speech, evaluation and topics contests? Additionally, who would win each of the District's trophies (Ace of Clubs, Moscow '93 Trophy, President's Award, Brian Driscoll Trophy) which now also included the Trevor Havelock award, presented to honour one of the District's 'greats' who sadly had passed away. The first award of that particular trophy went jointly to Vince Stevenson – then the District Development Officer – and Ian Price, both of the Speakers of Bromley Speakers Club. We could not know at that time that only two or three years later there would be serious dissension and also that the Bromley club would be expelled from ASC.

As District President, I found myself once again a member of NEC. I was allotted to the Education Committee which was led by the National Education Officer Joe James. I recall a good cooperative atmosphere as we worked our way through the always very busy agenda of items such as reviewing and improving the contest materials and modifying other printed items.

ASC's National President during that year was Brian Carter. At times he might appear to some to be slightly pedantic or even a little abrasive, but that was not the Brian Carter whom I got to know during the year. There was, however, one serious dispute in his year of leading ASC. This was the decision made by Brian Carter and endorsed by a vote of all the NEC members to change the Editor of The Speaker. The reason had been the unwillingness of the then Editor to publish some items requested by National Officers. The instruction therefore given to the deposed Editor was not to publish the next scheduled issue. However to everyone's surprise, an unofficial issue was printed and circulated by the ex-Editor. But the dust blew over and, in the end, the new Editor was duly appointed and the matter was settled.

This new editor was Irene Dick from near Glasgow. Her view was that the ASC's mouthpiece, The Speaker, should be "bigger than ASC" and thus have more of a PR impact for ASC as well as being just an internal house magazine. This was a sentiment that was near to my own way of thinking and led to contributions from such well-known figures as Esther Rantzen and Christine Hamilton in Irene's first issue, with more to follow in future issues.

On the Friday evening of one NEC meeting, the discussion between the various District Presidents who were present turned to suggesting some ideas for the future. It was a good opportunity to find out if some of the thoughts that we in South Eastern District had discussed two or three years before might possibly be shared by others. I remained fairly unspecific in what I said, especially since we had agreed in our earlier small group that what we were considering would be kept confidential. No very definite views emerged from my fellow District Presidents. However I believe that it was that evening's chat which led a year or two later to the re-opening of those earlier ideas on a larger scale.

In addition to life in the District and my duties at NEC, there were of course the two national speakers club events to attend and enjoy every year. One of these was the National Conference which every two or three years would give me a delightful excuse for visiting somewhere in Scotland. Sandra Barton, who was National President at the time of the 2003 conference in Dunblane, expressed it well when she wrote in her final report "Many people belong to our Association for the fun, pleasure and friendship they gain. This is our true spirit. We are here to share a hobby and enjoy time together". The other national event every year was the Speaker of the Year dinner. In Sandra's presidential year, ASC's Speaker of the Year was the Falklands hero, Simon Weston. Held in Cardiff, it was another memorable occasion, and I make no excuses for quoting Sandra's words once again, this time from her report appearing in The Speaker: "The secure handshake from those burnt and scarred hands set the sincerity for the evening".

Those early post-millennium years were marked for me by other happenings too. For example, Horsham District's Arts Fanfare festival came to a close in 2004. It had always received a very helpful grant from the West Sussex District Council. However council policy changed, the grant ceased, and we all took the sad decision to end what had been a highly popular feature of Horsham and West Sussex life for a dozen years. I continued as President of the local Muse & Music Society (founded of course by the very much lamented Jim Johnston) for a period of time, but I ceased holding this role after a further two or three years.

Another happening of that time was that, with the age of 70 fast approaching, I gradually ceased my full-time professional working life. I certainly appreciate that, for many people, retirement is indeed a time when you can claim to be "Free at last!" For many of us, however, we soon get the impression of being busier than ever and wondering how on earth we had ever managed to fit a 9-to-5 job into our life. I myself have that impression. Nevertheless, with final retirement approaching, I started to consider the possibility of advancing further within the Association, and submitted my application to be considered for the post of National Vice-President. This was confirmed and I was delighted to become the official nominee for that post in April 2006.

But meanwhile there was something else which was starting to exercise my mind more and more. This was the difficult situation of ASC – no longer simply its lack of growth, and slight decline in membership, but also the threat caused by its quickly growing rival – the Toastmasters.

One further event occurred, and this was an important one. I mentioned earlier my chat about possible development ideas in an informal District Presidents discussion evening at NEC. It was Keith Fraser, who by then was set to become National President, who recalled that discussion and suggested that I should share views with ASC's new Webmaster from Glasgow, Keir Smart. Keith had been struck by Keir's lively new ideas, and felt that discussion between the two of us might well be productive.

I finally met Keir for a meeting in a hotel in London, and was duly impressed. He was passionate about speaking, and especially the role of ASC in this regard. He had recently become a Trustee of the Speakers Trust (to which I shall return later in the final chapter of this memoir), and I found his web ideas most stimulating. The coming of IT was providing not merely administration benefits but also new opportunities for ASC, especially in respect of training, publicity and even sales of items. For instance he could envisage creating a range of DVDs for training, even extending to a 'virtual club', or possibly adding a commercial arm that might market ASC training books or similar.

The outcome of the meeting was that Keir set up a separate website for a small group of would-be "movers and shakers" who originally consisted of Keir, Irene Dick, Vince Stevenson, Debra Owen-Hughes, Dilwyn Scott and myself. It would be separate from the ASC website, but we would make contact when results emerged that would clearly benefit ASC.

Through our communications with each other via the website, we soon realised some similarities of the ideas of this new group to those of the informal group that had disbanded several years before. Concentrating on the recruitment need. Building a strong position with employers and getting their backing for their employees to join ASC. Achieving this by using the training strengths of various ASC members, and thus also achieving income for ASC. Starting in the south-east and then extending northwards. Managing the process by a body separate from ASC, with the intention of moving to joint control and management once it was proceeding successfully.

We felt it important that there should be some form of contact with NEC as we proceeded to plan. With this in mind, I myself was invited to attend with Keir an NEC meeting in June 2005 in Carlisle. I gave an outline presentation of what was being developed and why, who was involved, and the financial and membership benefits that might be expected in the first two or three years. The reception was encouraging, which was reassuring.

Development could now speed ahead. Sadly we lost Keir Smart, who needed to resign for personal reasons. However we gained some new participants, amongst whom was Mike Douse, and quite soon the development stage had reached the following key points:
- we would plan to launch in 2006, targeting mainly employers
- the 'product' would only be training, certainly initially
- the portfolio would include both speaking training and 'training the trainer', hopefully with some form of accreditation
- a new company was formed with, as Directors, Vince Stevenson, Dilwyn Scott, Gwyneth Millard and myself
- the new venture would bear the name College of Public Speaking, which rapidly became known by its abbreviation 'CoPS'.

In April 2006, I had the honour of being elected to the position of National Vice-President of ASC, and a new phase of my speaking journey began. There was much to do, which I shall describe in the next chapter, but meanwhile I'll continue with the CoPS story which was proceeding strongly.

The actions leading up to the 2006 launch were many and complex, as anyone who has brought out a new product – let alone a new company – will know full well. For instance, a website had to be commissioned and developed. Courses were designed, and one of these was piloted with a small banking group. Accreditation possibilities had to be explored. Financial arrangements had to be fully set up. Clubs within the south-east needed to be briefed on how they might hope to benefit. There were legal formalities plus, of course, numerous meetings to be arranged. However all was accomplished, and the launch could take place.

Some of the events of that year stand out. One of these was the College of Public Speaking's stand at a major exhibition in the ExCel Conference Centre in Docklands, which produced both some Press attention and useful contacts. Another was a mailing to the HR departments of some 200 concerns in the south-east. These produced a number of leads, of which one in particular stands out. This was a reply from the relevant department in Buckingham Palace, who have continued to use the services of CoPS regularly to the present day for the speaking training of curating and other staff.

An important activity during that launch year was the considerable presentation training help given by CoPS to one or two departments of British Telecom who, thanks to the efforts of the 2007 National Conference Convenor, Keith Dickerson, had agreed to provide substantial sponsorship support for ASC's forthcoming National Conference at a Hammersmith hotel. The staff training given by CoPS was a part-payment for this.

Finally, and possibly most importantly, CoPS provided its first donation to ASC. This was for £2000, and it was expected to be the first of many. But then, alas, some time before the end of my Vice-Presidential year, this potential part-solution to ASC's serious development problem came to a sudden and very unexpected end.

The evident need for CoPS and its development to be kept separate from the mainstream ASC development had been clear from the beginning, since the needs and procedures of one were so different from those of the other. Thus the product had to be launched and the benefits to ASC clearly had to start emerging before a sensible agreement between ASC and the CoPS operation could be drafted. This was, however, a real Achilles heel for the undertaking.

We had tried to offset any risk by giving the earlier presentation to NEC, by sending an information pamphlet to all clubs and, of course, by various conversations, but this proved insufficient. Very serious misgivings were expressed by some persons, and action needed to be taken urgently. Tony Coleman, who was the National President, therefore took that action, and called a Special Meeting of the NEC.

Some of the concerns expressed were entirely reasonable and could be discussed. For example the issue of conflict-of-interest was raised for me personally, since I was now Vice-President and, in all probability, I would shortly become ASC's National President. Standing down from being a Director of College of Public Speaking was my immediate solution for this fully-accepted problem. Another issue was the fact that the CoPS trainer (probably an ASC member) providing a CoPS course to a paying client, whether corporate or not, would need to be paid a normal corporate rate for the job. This was inevitable but was found unacceptable by a few persons.

Unfortunately however there had also been, both at the meeting and separately, certain personal and extremely unpleasant attacks on the integrity of some of us who were part of the venture. The animosity shown could lead to only one possible outcome. This was for the College of Public Speaking to separate entirely from any connection with the ASC, despite the purpose for which it had been created. All mentions of ASC, including the advice to follow up the training course by joining an ASC club, were removed from publicity material. Dilwyn, Gwyneth and I – as NEC officers – resigned as CoPS Directors and a new Board was installed. Most damagingly of all, the fundamental aim of all CoPS activity changed from benefiting ASC financially and numerically to benefiting only CoPS itself.

And thus, as I began my presidential year, I/we would have to start again in planning how to defend the situation of ASC against declining club numbers and the rapid advance of Toastmasters.

Chapter 6

Wearing the Chain

As I mentioned a little earlier, it was on a Saturday afternoon in April 2006 that I had the honour of being elected as National Vice-President of the Association of Speakers Clubs, and could look forward to receiving the senior chain of office in a year's time. A new stage of my speakers club life was very obviously starting.

I did not have long to wait for the first duty. This was the traditional task of running the National Evaluation Contest final on the Sunday morning of conference. It was a very good contest, well won by Lorna Scott-Dodd. To fill in the 8 minutes slot whilst the contestants were preparing their evaluations, I recalled the 'soundbite' talk given by Roger King MP a few years previously, and challenged some of the audience members to give a 15 to 30 second response to a question. I am pleased to say that the event went off smoothly. But once the conference had ended, I had to think matters through more carefully. What were in fact the duties of the Vice-President?

They appeared to me to be five in number. These were:

1. to stand in for the President, Tony Coleman, as and when required
2. to undertake any specific tasks given to me by the President
3. to learn the job of President
4. to plan for my own year as President
5. to decide on my Speaker of the Year

Starting at duty number one, there were very few occasions when I needed to stand in for Tony. One of these was an NEC meeting when for personal reasons he had to depart before Saturday's business began, and I had my first experience in the NEC chair. However the occasion that I particularly remember was the 90th birthday celebration held by Perth Speakers Club for ASC's Life Member, Kenneth McLeod Lewison. Tony had already accepted another invitation for that evening and was therefore unable to attend. I was most happy to stand in for him since Ken and I had become warm friends and had shared many a wee glass of malt both in meetings and at his home since that first encounter in Swindon some 20 years before.

I was also most happy to be given two specific tasks by the President. It had become clear that the publicity side of ASC needed to be strengthened both at the club level and at regional or national level. For this reason a Media Officer (later changed to a PR Officer) would be sought, and I was asked to prepare the job spec. The post would involve not merely seeking to raise ASC's profile, but also providing PR guidance to clubs. The search proved successful, and Mike Douse was appointed.

The other task assigned to me, which was to make new arrangements for ASC's archives, was also most interesting. For several years, one of the tasks undertaken by Ken Lewison was that of ASC archivist. In practice the archives were a large and bulky collection of both documents and miscellaneous trophies or regalia, much of it dating from Toastmaster days before 1971. All this was located up a ladder in Ken's attic which, by this time of his life, was clearly inappropriate.

It was Lorna Scott-Dodd, who was the daughter of ASC's first archivist – the late Maurice Scott-Dodd – who introduced me to another member, Sharron McColl, who was a librarian and archivist by profession. Sharron agreed to take over the archives, to expand them as necessary and to catalogue them electronically. Transport was arranged, and the problem satisfactorily solved.

The NEC (National Executive Committee) enjoyed a constructive year in 2006/7, well handled by Tony Coleman. As his Vice-President, I was in a good position to learn. For instance, NEC's Development Committee, led by National Development Officer Rosemary Harris, was especially productive. Not only was it a busy year with roadshows, 'taster' events and quite a number of new and useful guides, but Rosemary also created and sent a development questionnaire to all clubs to ascertain in detail their requirements.

Dilwyn Scott's Education Committee was also busy, including in its programme the creation of a list of tutorials and of persons experienced in delivering them.

With the departure of Keir Smart, a new Webmaster was needed, and Brian Micklethwaite took over this role in September 2006. The website was largely refashioned and updated. Brian particularly acknowledged the help given by Croydon's Peter Curtis-Allen whose company Net Services International gave much help in its hosting of the site and in developing the national database of speakers clubs. Brian also planned such innovations as a discussion forum and a "website of the month" feature.

My year as Vice-President also gave me the opportunity to get close to the financial aspects of ASC. For instance there were issues to discuss such as a new mileage rate, new signatories for the accounts, the size of the Association's reserve, and even additions to the list of materials, such as ASC umbrellas and ASC rucksacks. One factor which appeared to be increasingly a problem was the question of cost, especially as there was inevitably resistance to increasing the member's capitation fee level. For example, at club level, room-hire costs had increased for many clubs. At the national level, hotel costs for the National Conference and the expense costs for NEC meetings were now greater than in the past. The first voices started to be raised suggesting totally radical solutions, such as turning National Conference into a one-day meeting and even ceasing to publish our house magazine, The Speaker. When my Vice-Presidential year began, it was reassuring to know that the financial problem should be eased by the advent of the College of Public Speaking, since its profits would be passed to the ASC. But then came the special meeting – described in the previous chapter – and the decision to separate CoPS from ASC completely. Thus the financial problem would remain to be solved.

This brings me to the next task for my Vice-Presidential year. The Presidency is an honorary position, which includes being a figurehead. But it is also – within ASC – a chief executive and 'buck stops here' position, fully responsible for the overall management of ASC during the year of office. This necessarily implied some form of advance planning.

Regarding the issue of planning for the year ahead, it was clear what my priority should be. ASC, with all its great story, was facing severe challenges. Instead of the anticipated steady growth, decline had started to set in. Moreover, instead of being alone in the speakers club marketplace, a very large competitor – Toastmasters – was gaining ground, primarily in the south-east. So the priority could not be a simple one of administration or of cost-cutting. It would of necessity have to be marketing-centred and strategically-based.

My final key task in my year as National Vice-President was to decide on my year's Speaker of the Year and to put in hand the organisation of the Award Dinner. This all had to be planned in advance since ASC's tradition was that the Speaker of the Year Dinner would take place before Christmas.

Since its inception, the Speaker of the Year promotion and in particular the gala dinner had become an exciting part of ASC's annual calendar. Promotionally it had the potential to be a great publicity story for ASC. Some members had at times expressed disappointment since the PR potential had not in fact often being tapped. But that of course was up to us – the clubs – and not up to our chosen Speaker of the Year, whose part of the bargain was simply to accept the title and to attend and speak at the dinner. Nevertheless in some cases – and here I refer particularly to Edwina Currie and later to Jack Webster - the Speaker of the Year might well wish to find out more about ASC and even visit one or two clubs.

There was no fixed method of choosing the Speaker of the Year. Different methods had been used over time, including actual polling amongst all clubs. The method which I decided upon was to discuss the possibilities initially with my own two clubs. As a result, we arrived at a short list of 4 very interesting candidates. These were the Most Rev John Sentamu, Archbishop of York, (Lord) Digby Jones – ex-Director-General of the CBI, the remarkable (and profoundly deaf) percussionist Evelyn Glennie, and the greatly popular BBC weather forecaster Carol Kirkwood. To avoid possible disappointments later, I contacted each and was assured that they would be willing to accept the honour and attend a dinner.

I then checked out the four possibilities with my fellow NEC members, and received approval. I was also pleased to discover that my own preference, which was for the Archbishop of York, appeared to appeal slightly more to those with whom I discussed the matter, and I therefore invited him. Our invitation was accepted, and we now, for the first time, had an Archbishop as our Speaker of the Year. The other three candidates were quite happy to accept that they had been "beaten by an Archbishop" when I rang, and we remained on good terms. As described in the next chapter, this proved to be fortuitous in one case!

The next stage was to meet and fix all the details with the Archbishop's team. This involved two long meetings in Bishopthorpe, which was the Archbishop's historic Palace near York, and one or two meetings in York itself, where York Speakers Club's Clive Dawson – Eastern District President the year before – gallantly stepped up to the plate and took on the demanding role of Dinner Organiser.

All in all, therefore, my year as National Vice-President had been busy and had prepared me well for my own term as National President.

The National Conference at which I would receive the chain of office took place in the final week of April 2007 in the Novotel West London Hotel in the London Borough of Hammersmith. I recall it as an excellent conference, very well organised by Keith Dickerson and his team. The proceedings started on Friday evening with the Final of the National Topics Contest and continued on the Saturday morning with the annual meeting of General Council, which was the culminating function of Tony Coleman's year as National President. The Final of the National Speech Contest – won by Wimbledon's Michael Ronayne, who went on to win it two further times – then followed in the normal way.

It was following the Final of the National Speech Contest that Tony passed over to me the National President's Chain of Office and my own term started. My initial duties were the customary ones of presenting my predecessor with his Past President's purple tie, introducing Joe James of Tyneside Speakers Club as my National Vice-President, and welcoming to the podium the 8 District Presidents who would be taking office for 2007/8.

Saturday evening was the occasion for the Annual Gala Dinner, in which I would make the first speech of many as the Association's National President. I had invited Joan Milburn to MC the event, Giles Robinson of Chaucer Club to propose the Toast to the Guests and my ex-Redhill & Reigate colleague David Whitmore to respond, and Mike Douse to propose the Toast to the Association to which I would respond.

The weekend concluded with the Sunday morning interfaith service led by David Whitmore (who was a lay reader) and the National Final of the Evaluation Contest chaired by Joe James. My year had now really started.

The principal administrative task of the National President is to be the executive head of ASC for one year. This involves chairing the three meetings of the National Executive Committee (NEC) in June, October and February, plus the General Council meeting of all the clubs in the Association at the end of April. Over the years, I had become used to how NEC worked in those days (and mainly still continues to work), but readers may find a few words of explanation useful.

For a start, the basic membership of the National Executive Committee consists of 15 members. These are:

The 7 National Officers (viz. national president / national vice–president / immediate past national president / national secretary / national treasurer / national development officer / national education officer)
The 8 District Presidents of the Association.

To these may be added the Minutes Secretary (who attends all meetings) plus any of the following national officers who may be invited for a specific meeting – Webmaster, Conference Convenor, Materials Officer, Editor of The Speaker, Archivist.

Committee meetings form part of each NEC meeting. At the start of the year, 4 of the District Presidents are allocated to the National Development Officer's Development Committee, and the other 4 are allocated to the National Education Officer's Education Committee. Whilst those two committees are meeting, the remaining members present attend the President's Committee. (In addition, a Constitutional Committee, a Nominations Committee and an informal Conference Action Group also exist.)

All NEC members, both National and District, submit a report prior to each NEC meeting. Thus for my first meeting, which was held in Birmingham in June 2007, we already had a variety of matters to consider.

A principal one of these was finance since, despite the sponsorship of BT, the recent National Conference had incurred a 5-figure loss. The main reason for this was that the numbers attending had been lower than predicted, which meant that the number of hotel rooms actually occupied was significantly lower than those which had been guaranteed for our use by the hotel and would thus still have to be paid for. Fortunately this loss did not put the overall financial situation of ASC at risk but the problem certainly had to be confronted. Partly thanks to the training of the BT 'management pool' carried out by CoPS, BT agreed to help with further sponsorship for the following year, whilst another part of the solution was for the National Treasurer to be part of the conference planning team in future years, especially at the time when the agreement was made with the chosen hotel. Nevertheless – and disappointingly for we Londoners – the higher costs associated with London events meant that the NEC was less likely to hold events in London in the future.

Another unfortunate issue, also emanating from the South Eastern District, started to raise its head and indeed continued to be present for several years. Not surprisingly, some members of speakers clubs are in fact full- or part-time professional speaking trainers. These would, for example, have formed much of the resource for the work originally intended to be carried out for ASC by the College of Public Speaking. Most regrettably, serious dissension had broken out between two senior South Eastern District club members regarding the professional training issue which carried right through into dissension within ASC itself. This problem also was discussed – though not solved – in June's NEC meeting. Overall, however, the committee meetings and the general forum meetings of the NEC proved both positive and productive throughout the whole year.

Let me take the National Education Committee as an example. An early task of that committee was to review the recent contests and if necessary improve them for the future. Microphone use was a case in point. Some speakers had started to dispense with the use of the lectern and instead address the audience more directly. Hence the provision of lapel microphones was becoming more necessary. Another issue concerned the increasing importance of training. Easily the principal reason why people come along to a speakers club in the first place is to improve their speaking, both in standard and in confidence. Hence training, whether through a tutorial, a course, or possibly a seminar, was increasingly seen as a truly vital task. National Education Officer Dilwyn Scott therefore put training as the priority for his committee during the year, and also suggested the possible appointment of a National Training Officer by ASC.

Particularly impressive was the programme of work that was being carried out by National Development Officer Rosemary Harris and her committee. It was Rosemary's strong belief that her committee's task was to provide the tools whereby clubs could build their membership, including starting new clubs. Thus a wide variety of printed materials plus actual roadshows and taster sessions flowed from her productive mind. As she herself wrote in an article in The Speaker towards the end of her time in the post, "When I started two years ago, I believed that, if members were provided with the tools to "develop" clubs, success would follow. That has taken time, but there are signs that the strategy is working.......I know that I am leaving the Association with a legacy that I am proud of".

My own priority for my first NEC meeting was to introduce a Framework Planning Document for the year. Summarising briefly, it stated (i) that no major changes in administration were envisaged, (ii) that concentration on the very important issue of training would be given, and (iii) most important of all, that the long-standing decline in numbers absolutely had to be reversed, and growth in both club and member numbers had to be achieved. This implied an emphasis on strategic and tactical planning at all levels, and I was pleased to see that virtually all NEC members backed this approach wholeheartedly.

Thus my task for the year was clear. It had been a successful and encouraging first meeting.

Most speakers clubs take a break during the summer, my own included. Nevertheless there was much to do. An early task was to seek to spend some time talking with NEC members and gaining their views. Mike Douse, for example, had taken on PR responsibility and was certainly full of remarkably good ideas. Could we not start making approaches to influence the government on the vital need for children to learn speaking at school? Or develop possibilities for speaking to be somehow associated with the Olympic Games which were going to be held in London in a few years' time? And a closer link with Rotary's annual "Youth Speaks" contest would prove beneficial, as might an Internet-based evaluation contest, if it could be imagined.

Other conversations covered different subjects. Succession planning must always be a consideration in any organisation, and I was particularly pleased to realise that Rosemary Harris was not averse to a possible nomination for National Vice-President. Soon after this she was in fact selected as the NEC nominee, and I was disappointed when finally, at the start of 2008, she decided not to pursue that ambition after all. National Secretary Gwyneth Millard, who was a central figure to whom I needed to talk at least once a week, was another who had branched out, including taking on some outside training assignments and starting a new speakers club at Standish.

Another task which I had set myself was to have an hour or two's meeting with each of the ASC's 8 District Presidents for the coming year. This I was able to do between July and September. Many miles of travelling were of course involved, and the conversations were held in venues ranging from pubs and private homes to mainline railway stations. However the results were most revealing and worthwhile. Both problems and opportunities showed up strongly. For some, the main problem was the lack of candidates wishing to take office. For others, a larger problem was that of steadily ageing clubs. At the same time, there were mentions of provisional plans for new speakers clubs. North Western District's Graham McLachlan, for example, shared with me his plan for starting two more clubs and for the growth of his district membership to 250.

The end result was not merely my own increased knowledge and hopefully more trust between each of us, but also a clear idea of how the detailed planning which I was intending might work. What I came to see as "district powerhouses" would help form the background and basis for future strategy.

Meanwhile the other principal task of a presidential year was also starting to take shape. This was the key figurehead role of attending speakers club dinners. For many if not most speakers clubs, their annual dinner is the centrepiece event of the year. It is the occasion when the social side of the club truly comes into its own. As well as their own members' guests, clubs may well decide to invite representatives from other clubs, from their Area or District, or even National officers to the dinner. I, like my predecessors and those who have followed me, received numerous invitations to club dinners during the year. It is the duty (a very pleasant duty, I should add) of the National President to accept the invitations whenever possible.

The format is similar in most cases. It is an occasion for after-dinner speeches which, for many years, appeared as Level B9 in the Speakers Guide (now replaced by a 'rapport' speech). The programme will customarily take the form of Toasts - perhaps to the club: perhaps to the guests: and in most cases to the Association. The National President, if invited, would reply to the Toast to the Association.

As I say, representing the Association on these occasions is both an honour and privilege, and I was asked to undertake almost two dozen dinners – at least one in every one of ASC's 8 Districts – during my time as National President and the year before. Thankfully speech preparation seems to take less time as one's experience grows.

Some of these dinners were bound to stand out more than others. There was for instance the dinner marking the 50th Anniversary of Morecambe Speakers Club. Morecambe has historical significance for ASC since it was in that club's normal meeting room that the meeting was held in November 1971 which took the decision to start ASC as an independent organisation.

Another Dinner was particularly memorable for a different reason. This was the annual dinner held in Ythan, which is a small town on the road running north from Aberdeen towards Peterhead. I remember that area of the coast well, partly because I came across a large seal colony, and partly because America's Donald Trump was seeking to convert a large expanse of unspoiled coast into a holiday resort for the very affluent. The welcome was as always most warm. However I particularly recall the occasion because, while we were eating, I checked with my hostess that I should speak for the normal 10 to 15 minutes and to my alarm received the response "Oh no – you are our chief guest and we expect the chief guest to address us for 30 or 40 minutes!". I am pleased to say that I did in fact speak for just over 30 minutes. But there was more to follow.

Having sat down I was assured that my speech had gone down well. I was also informed that it had compared satisfactorily with the speech of the previous year's chief guest who – much to my surprise – turned out to have been Alec Salmond!

Not all invitations were to attend a dinner. Towards the end of my year of office, several of the invitations were to attend a District's annual conference which included its annual speaking contests. I would be quite likely to find myself being chief judge in the afternoon, and the skills of many contestants never ceased to amaze me.

But it was a completely different type of event entirely which perhaps made the strongest impression on me during my travels in that year. It had been the practice of Greenock and neighbouring clubs to host a primary school speech contest for schools on both sides of the River Clyde. I have frequently attended speaking functions among young people in secondary schools but not amongst those under 10 years of age. The fluency and the lack of fear of these very young contestants was breathtaking and reinforced my view that we in ASC have a part to play in society that is wider than simply communicating with our own members.

Meanwhile one key event of the year was fast approaching. This was the Speaker of the Year Dinner scheduled to take place in York on Saturday 17th November. Clive Dawson and his team had indeed worked hard during this time. The arrangements at the venue had been completely organised, all ASC clubs had been fully informed, attendance targets had been reached, and the trophy had been manufactured and delivered.

I followed the traditional guidelines in preparing the programme for the evening. The first speech would be the Toast to the Guests, which Past National President Bill Mitchell kindly agreed to give. The response would be given by Sue Warner, founder of Speakers Bank and now a Trustee of the Speakers Trust. It would be my duty to propose the Toast and present the Award to the Archbishop of York, Most Rev John Sentamu, our Speaker of the Year, following which he would give his speech. The proceedings would end with a Vote of Thanks to be given by Denise Adlard, President of Eastern District.

I have always enjoyed adding an unexpected item or 'a piece of theatre' to any event or programme which I have run, and one possibility existed for this Dinner. To explain it, I need to go back in history. Firstly by about 20 years, and secondly much further in time.

It was about 20 years earlier that the infamous Idi Amin came to power in the East African country of Uganda. It did not take long before his rule became both autocratic and somewhat bizarre. Over the years, a sizeable Indian community had taken root in Uganda, and in many ways they had become the kingpins of the Ugandan economy. So there was no apparent logic in the fact that Idi Amin started to persecute the Indian community. One of those imprisoned by the dictator was our forthcoming Speaker of the Year who had been highly trained initially in law. In his own words, he had been "kicked about like a football" by Idi Amin's people, but was eventually allowed to leave and come to Britain where he had taken a different vocation and was now the second highest figure in the Church of England. Finally, of course, the whole Indian community of Uganda was expelled, many came to Britain, and undoubtedly Uganda's loss had been Britain's gain.

Going back further in time – right back to colonial days in the 40s – ASC's long-serving life member Ken Lewison had moved from being a member of the Long Range Desert Patrol in the Sahara to serving as a Lieutenant Colonel in the King's African Rifles Regiment in East Africa. He had once described to me the time when three new recruits were paraded before him. Two of them were low in stature, while the third was both tall and bulky. And the name of that one – Idi Amin! Ken recounted how they served their "apprenticeship" in the regiment, and how Idi Amin advanced quite quickly through to officers training school and eventually beyond.

I therefore thought for a time of including a short "memoir" speech by Ken Lewison talking about that initial encounter in Uganda. It would probably have qualified as "good theatre", but a second opinion was clearly needed. Thus, after talking it over with the Archbishop's chaplain, I went no further.

The reason was that the Archbishop's experience of that cruel figure Idi Amin was far too 'raw', and the result of including such an item in the programme would have been much too uncomfortable.

Finally the day of the Speaker of the Year Dinner arrived, and all arrangements worked well. We had earlier asked the Archbishop to nominate a charity that would benefit from a raffle. His nominations were for the East Window Fund for York Minster and for the St Martin's Hospice in the York area. I am pleased to say that sizeable donations were given to both. It was certainly an unforgettable joy for me and my partner to be able to spend the whole evening in conversation with someone whom I so greatly admired, and with his wife. It was particularly pleasurable to listen to his speech in which he expressed both his passion and his compassion. I had asked him to talk for some 20 to 25 minutes, which he did, and in that time we could all fully realise why he was indeed our Speaker of the Year. In fact the only negative comment for the whole event that I received was a wish that I should have asked him to speak for somewhat longer!

Meanwhile I'll return to the "management progress" of the year, which had been proceeding well. All National Presidents doubtless have an aim for their year of office. Mine, as I have stated, was to seek to halt the decline in clubs and members, and to start the creation of growth. No longer would this be aided by the CoPS venture. Instead a totally new strategy and plan would be needed. My initial thought was for the drafting of this plan to be carried out by a drafting group but, on consideration, it became clear that few members – especially at NEC level - had acquired this marketing planning type of experience. Moreover one senior member, who had in fact been my first choice to include in the drafting group, turned out to have a completely different view. His wish was to simplify ASC and to return it to consisting of almost 'stand-alone' independent clubs with few if any national aspirations.

I decided instead to carry out most of the drafting of the paperwork myself since, after all, developing marketing plans and strategy had been my career throughout my working life and, additionally, I already had over 25 years ASC experience. The all-important role of the clubs and the NEC members would be to comment in detail, to revise and improve what had been put down, or possibly to disagree and give their own thoughts.

October's NEC meeting and indeed the later Spring 2008 meeting were once again remarkably positive. Yet again we had the benefit of the reports which both District Officers and National Officers had prepared. It was abundantly clear that there was a common factor, which was that all clubs badly wanted to have new and especially young blood. One report commented on there being some 'clubs waiting to die', and two others referred to a shortage of people putting themselves forward for office. Another report mentioned the rather sad story of a speakers club which had decided to become mixed and 'as a result lost several members'.

This is not to say that there were no encouraging items. For instance, the in-house club which Rosemary was trying to develop in Solihull Hospital was proceeding and, thought Rosemary, might even lead to other NHS clubs. A Scottish District report referred to the development of a Probus (i.e. retired persons) club in one town, whilst another noted interest in starting a club within the Isle of Man.

The National Officers' reports were also of interest. The Constitutional Committee was looking at developing new Model Rules for clubs. The Webmaster noted that the number of clubs with a website had risen to some 68, and he was investigating areas such as PayPal. Dilwyn Scott, National Education Officer, commented that he personally had carried out over a dozen training seminars in different parts of the country. The Archivist reported having spent 100 hours already since her appointment, and that 'the future is digitalisation', whilst Mike Douse, as PR officer, had now prepared his promised "Strike a Happy Medium" guide for clubs to use.

Looking back at my own pre-meeting reports for our October meeting and later for our February meeting, I see that I had made various visits and also that I had circulated such items as a guide to the "pre-meeting course" which had consistently helped to build new clubs and club members, and a "club self-assessment" document which had received favourable comments.

It was particularly encouraging that the NEC continued to be fully supportive of the development of the medium-term strategy for the ASC. The meeting in February 1988 was of the greatest significance. By this time, the medium-term plan was fully in place. The ASC situation was now detailed both in words and in figures, a full SWOT (i.e. strengths/weaknesses/opportunities/threats) analysis existed, the objectives were stated, and the strategy and tactics for achieving them were completely documented.

The final proposal also included two important appendices. One of these was a specimen framework for a district plan which it was hoped that other districts might copy. It had been prepared in full consultation with the South Western District President Noel Collins, who thoroughly appreciated the need for ASC to get its act together. The other appendix was a description of how Toastmasters were rapidly expanding in the south-east, and why they were succeeding so well. In brief, it would appear to be because Toastmasters was goal-orientated whereas ASC was primarily skill-orientated. For this I had to thank the great help of Ipswich's James McGinty who, as well as his office in ASC, was – like three or four other south-east ASC members – an office-holder within Toastmasters International.

It would have been surprising if no counter-views had been received, and in fact there were two of significance. The first of these centred on one of the eight strategic principles, which urged ASC to be cooperative with other bodies to achieve more status and better results. For example Speakers Trust and the University of the Third Age were amongst the links I had mentioned. A surprisingly negative view was put forward from one source that links of this type should always be avoided since they could lead to less transparency, mixed objectives and so on. ASC should "stand alone" whatever the potential benefits.

The second counter-view was of more significance. This was the argument that the strategy and plan as written were too ambitious for the ASC, since the clubs and the members were untrained for this purpose. This was a realistic objection. It was already clear to me that the question of implementation would have to be thoroughly addressed. There was also awareness that we had to overcome the planning problem that naturally arises from the fact that a National President has only one year in office before handing over.

Overall, however, the medium-term strategy document was warmly welcomed and it was agreed that it should now be put forward to General Council. The basis on which it would be put forward in April was particularly democratic. It would be presented almost as a draft for all clubs to consider and possibly revise. It would then be brought back to General Council for final approval as ASC policy the following year.

That final NEC meeting of my presidential year covered many other points too. A particularly important one was a proposal put forward by my predecessor, Tony Coleman, to fully revise the NEC meetings method, partly for cost reasons – partly for greater effectiveness. The proposal put forward by Tony was to remove the overnight element almost completely (i.e. to have single-day meetings), and to limit attendance at the three meetings per year to the regular members of the President's Committee. Meanwhile the Development and Education Committees, each of which consisted of a National Officer and 4 District Presidents) would make their own arrangements for meetings. By this means there would be a great reduction in costs and also the advantage of these two basic committees not being confined just to meeting three times a year on the Saturday morning.

After discussion, it was fully agreed that Tony's proposal too would go ahead to General Council in April.

Preparation for the annual meeting of General Council, which is only one element of a very full weekend of events, is highly complex. Certainly it involves the Conference Convenor and the organising team. Added to this are the secretarial side, the preparation of the NEC's executive report, which consists of reports from all National officers, the annual financial report, the detailed papers concerning apologies, expenses and the like, and the full detail of the agenda. The many papers sent or emailed out in advance to all clubs and other officers included the complete medium-term strategy document. However there was one final task to undertake before General Council at the end of April.

One of the realities of commercial life is that the best laid plans run the risk of being put on the shelf and never implemented. This risk had to be overcome, so four steps had to be put in hand. These were (i) the fullest possible briefing, (ii) a working group to control and carry out the implementation, (iii) systems for detailed monitoring of progress and, if possible, (iv) a detailed training programme to ensure that those responsible for implementation could and would do it.

In addition I felt that success would require each District taking on a 'powerhouse' role for implementation of the plan. It would certainly involve each District Council fully grasping the fact that its role was not simply to administer but to develop.

The first of these four steps duly took place – a day of briefing my successors fully. We booked a room in York for the day and went through how each step might be achieved. I have always been accused of writing too many wordy documents. On this occasion, the document we worked our way through had no fewer than 50 pages! Unfortunately, though, the next step, viz. my working party proposal, never went ahead. One possible reason for this was the fact the plan would still be seen as a draft for the next 12 months, and complete implementation could only be put in hand once it had been agreed with any revisions by the General Council meeting in the following year, 2009. This omission also extended to the plan to form a separate younger team for the purpose of recruiting strongly amongst those in their 20s and 30s, who were still less than 10% of the overall membership.

By this time, the date for the national conference at Blackpool was fast approaching. But there was one final hiccup to be overcome.

I mentioned earlier that the CoPS crisis of the year before, solved by separating CoPS completely from ASC, had led to dissensions within the South Eastern District that were to continue for several years to come. One specific previously unknown factor was suddenly brought to light the week before conference which could have caused us a serious problem. In the event, it was simply referred to NEC for action. Sadly, however, the final result of that factor was that it led in the end to some damaging expulsions from ASC.

National Conference finally arrived. This would be the last time that I would be wearing the chain of office, and I was determined to enjoy it. Everything clicked into place. It was an excellent Friday evening, which included the National Topics Contest final and also gave me the opportunity to hold a small reception for some of those who had been closest and most helpful during my year of office.

Then came the Saturday morning meeting of General Council. All National

Presidents have a feeling of apprehension as they are about to preside at this meeting and invariably give a sigh of relief when it passes off smoothly. I was no exception. It was then that I experienced the real value of the support team, especially the Minutes Secretary and the National Secretary. I had been provided by them with detailed instructions (referred to as "my idiots guide") to guide me through the agenda programme. For instance, each officer in General Council proposes that his or her report is accepted. However a seconder is needed – and that person's name was also in the "idiots guide". Another example was the handling of Motions, and especially any amendments. One of the great benefits of ASC membership is learning all aspects of chairmanship, and that learning is vital in the General Council meeting. I was particularly grateful to those who helped me to successfully accomplish the business of the meeting.

In the end the meeting went well. The Mayor duly arrived at 9.00 am as planned and welcomed us warmly to Blackpool. Then, at the fixed time for the AGM, the business itself began. The Minutes of the previous year's meeting and officers' reports – and even the financial report – proceeded smoothly. There was one question which referred to the South Eastern District problem, which was duly referred to the next meeting of the NEC. The nominated officers for the following year – Joe James, proposed by me as National President, and David Grainger, proposed by Hilary Hampshaw as National Vice-President, were duly elected.

We finally reached the point where I stepped down temporarily from chairing the meeting in order to become the proposer (seconded by Mike Douse) for the medium-term strategy Motion. The full wording was: "that General Council is pleased to receive the draft ASC strategy proposal and directs NEC to seek responses from as many members as possible, to take forward proposals where it is clearly appropriate to do so, and to return to General Council with any revisions to these proposals and with a report on progress in 2009". There was a useful discussion. A few points were raised from the floor. Finally the Motion was passed with only an extremely small number of those present opposing or abstaining. My main objective been achieved.

Matters thereafter followed their traditional course. The afternoon saw the final of the National Speech Contest – which for many is the real highlight of

ASC's annual conference - and soon it was time for my final duty of the year. This was, quite simply, to make a final statement to all present, and then to hand over the chain of office to Joe James, my extremely worthy successor.

For me, it had been a year that I shall always look back on with immense pleasure and even pride. I had met many people, made many speeches, presented many awards, and run many meetings. I had also, I believed, led the way in providing a strategy for the future which should benefit ASC for some years to come. It was time to return to a normal speakers club life.

Posing for a photograph on the evening of my inauguration as National President with Joe James, elected that afternoon as National Vice-President, and Joan Milburn, who kindly officiated as MC at that evening's gala dinner.

Meeting up again at a Cardiff dinner in my presidential year with Dennis Damond-John who had been present as a visitor in Cheltenham at my first-ever attendance at a speakers club.

A mixture of fancy and non-fancy attire at Camden Speakers Club's June 2009 party. From left to right, Gwyn Redgers, Debra Owen-Hughes, Deidre James. a Camden member and (Cardinal?) Joe James.)

Michael Ronayne of Wimbledon Speakers Club is here seen holding the trophy as the 2007 Winner of the ASC National Speech Competition. He later went on to win the award again on two further occasions.

Gwyn Redgers (National President) with ASC's 2007 Speaker of the Year - Most Reverend Dr John Sentamu (Archbishop of York) - and with Mrs Margaret Sentamu

Speaker of the Year - and the House of Commons - Betty Boothroyd MP (now Dame), with National President Peter Dawkins on her right and Tony Benn MP on her left, Tony Benn himself was to become ASC's Speaker of the Year in a later year.

Speakers Trust reception in the Speakers apartments in the Palace of Westminster. From left to right, Gwyn Redgers, The Speaker (John Bercow MP), Gwyneth Millard, Joe James (ASC National President)

Mike Douse (seated) and James McGinty (speaking) were two members of the ASC team in the College of Public Speaking's 'Speaking Olympiad' which I chaired in 2010 in The George Tavern in The Strand. Horsham's Barry Miles was the third member of the ASC team.

Members of CLDS debate training team in the IDebate Rwanda 2013 debate camp. From left to right, Jordan Anderson, Tony Koutsoumbos, Gwyn Redgers, Jack Watling

Students attending the IDebate Rwanda debate camp enjoying a break on the shore of Lake Milayi.

Chapter 7

My ASC club life continues

Leaving the presidency of ASC did not mean immediately vanishing from the NEC scene. Instead I would be holding for a year the title of Immediate Past National President, and in any case there was still the basic issue of medium-term strategy to pursue. So, in this account of my speakers club journey, I shall begin by continuing my NEC story before starting again on my club life story.

Within ASC, the National Presidency is a one year appointment only. My successor, Joe James, was a highly experienced and effective chairman of committees who needed little or no help from his predecessor. Thus, for me, 2008/9 was a more relaxing year. However there was one particular occasion, early in 2008, when the events of the year before helped save the day. It concerned the Speaker of the Year Dinner.

Speakers of the Year can at times charge highly for the talks they give to outside audiences. However they gave their services to ASC free in return for the title. At times, it is very clear that they would appreciate a contribution being made to a charity, and thus a number of Speaker of the Year Dinners (including mine in the previous year) have included raffles or other arrangements being made for charity donations. At other times this had not needed to happen.

Joe, like me, had been careful to sound out the likelihood that his preferred Speaker of the Year would accept the award, and would be prepared to come and speak at the dinner on the normal terms. However, very late in the day, it transpired that a misunderstanding had occurred and that Joe's first choice would be expecting a sizeable payment. It was very fortunate indeed that the discussions with Lord Digby Jones of a year previously (including advising him that he had been "beaten by an Archbishop") had been so positive that he was more than happy to be considered for this later year instead. Joe decided therefore to invite him, Digby accepted the invitation, and the resulting dinner was one of the most successful in the whole series, partly due to the fact that the Speaker of the Year happily went from table to table talking to people.

Meantime NEC activity continued positively. One of the tasks Joe had set himself was to ensure that the District level was strong and that communications were good between all levels of the Association, and this was happening. He had also needed to appoint some new National Officers to fill vacancies which had occurred, and this too happened. I particularly remember from that time the spread of new ideas relating to both the public relations and development side which flowed from the newly appointed Mike Douse in what he amusingly referred to as 'a smorgasbord of half-baked ideas'. Some early examples were contacts with both Parliament and with a TV film producer, a development newsletter, a virtual speaking contest, a proposed speakers bureau and even a contest to find a new and consumer-friendly name for ASC.

During my Immediate Past National President year, I had retained one specific task. This was to progress ASC's medium-term strategy from "draft" to "final approval". In the final AGM of my presidential year, the strategy had been welcomed and accepted by General Council. However the actual wording of the motion was to urge clubs to consider the strategy fully during the coming year and, if necessary, suggest amendments. Final approval would then hopefully take place at the 2009 AGM.

The full document had been mailed early in 2008 to every club and was now also available in complete detail on the ASC website. We had hoped that there would be a string of comments, whether positive or negative. In this we were to be disappointed. The only comments received had been the occasional notes of reinforcement or even praise about some aspect that had been written in the document. We had also hoped to get a discussion started in the columns of The Speaker. However the then Editor decided against giving space for that purpose. Thus, as the 2009 General Council meeting started to get closer, there were virtually no changes to be made.

For the General Council debate, delegates were reminded of the strategy by a card which highlighted The Vision, and The Route (i.e. the 8 strategy points) for achieving that vision. Seconded on this occasion by David Grainger, I proposed the motion "that General Council now endorses the ASC Strategy Proposal presented to it in 2008, and instructs NEC to manage and promote its implementation, guided by the ASC Constitution, reporting on progress annually to General Council". Once again, the Motion was passed with only the tiniest number of abstentions or rejections, which was good news. Sadly, however, my intended implementation task force was not created. Nevertheless I was hopeful that the strategy would bear fruit.

The first point of the 8-point strategy was "to ensure ASC's positioning as an authoritative leader in the development of speaking skills". Thus the club's training ability was central to the ASC proposition. In the course of discussion, the concept of having a Summer School for this purpose emerged, and plans were soon drafted. 2 or 3 people in Western District expressed particular interest and a provisional booking was therefore made to hold a "Summer Training Weekend" for 20 or so people in the University of Cumbria's Lancaster campus. This would focus primarily on Western District members, officers and "movers and shakers". However visitors from other Districts would be most welcome. The cost per person would be £125 and a draft programme for Friday evening to Sunday lunchtime was drawn up.

Unfortunately, despite the good early expressions of interest, the numbers actually confirming their attendance proved too low, and the event had to be cancelled. The reason given by several was that, as residents of Lancashire themselves (i.e. Western District), they could not see the point of paying for accommodation when they could have made the trip there and back in the day and slept at home! But perhaps a more basic reason, which on reflection augured badly for the future of the strategy, was a failure to see the importance of the training need. One or two other training events continued to take place, of course. For example Mike Douse organised development seminars which covered aspects of the strategy in Edinburgh and in an East Midlands airport location. However I myself continue to believe very strongly in the potential importance to ASC of holding a 2-3 day training event for the coming year's officers in the last two or three weeks before club meetings resume in September.

The other casualty of that period, to which I have already referred, was a most difficult situation within South Eastern District. It is never easy when friends fall out, but sadly this was the case in the south-east. Tensions continued to build up and deeply affected several clubs. It would take almost two more years before various enquiries were finalised, some club and member expulsions took place and the South Eastern District could once again start to settle down. One particular problem which resulted was that my own area, which was South Area, reduced from 5 clubs to 2 clubs, and this still remains the situation. A tentative chance of a club in Crawley, linked in with that town's Festival of Learning, failed to materialise.

Nevertheless in the District as a whole, there were also some good happenings. For instance, just 10 years after Debra Owen-Hughes had started the highly successful Wimbledon Speakers Club, she came up with another winner – the new Camden Speakers Club. It was certainly no surprise that, just 2-3 years later, Debra became the National Development Officer of the Association!

The fortunes of my own two clubs differed in some ways.

One of them, Redhill & Reigate, had become a successful club with 17 members at one stage. Members of the club, such as its founder Richard Kilroy, and the main mover at the start of ASC's website development - Feargal Hogan - were among those who had played vital roles. The annual dinners, at times held jointly with Horsham, had been excellent events. Additionally it was a club that was able to spring a surprise from time to time. Speakers club officers are well used to receiving memos referring to a forthcoming annual general meeting. But it was only the Redhill & Reigate club that, hearing about a Scottish club's earlier Mafia-inspired event, decided to follow suit. The result was a notice which I received (from 'Padrino' to 'Dear Capo') stating that "20 junio is AGM of Cosa Nostra Redhill. So do good report, compre? Family wanta the lowdown on profit and problemas. No stitcha the family up, OK", and so on.

Another very helpful step was that the club, after two or three moves, seemed to have found a very suitable venue. This was a function room of the Toby Carvery, just 200 yards up the hill from Redhill station. We were able to hold our meetings there, and, for several years to run our pre-meeting course.

However the management changed, and we were forced to confront no less than a doubling of our fortnightly rental. This was too much and we moved to a different venue, somewhat further from the town centre. The new venue was a church hall. It seemed pleasant enough, but unfortunately it seemed to be as a direct result of the move that club membership dropped in a few months to only about one half of its earlier number.

Two or three years later there was a reversal of this very swingeing rent charged by the Toby Carvery, and we have happily returned there. However, numbers have remained at the lower level of about 8 persons at the present time. Despite this, the club is still positively achieving its purpose and it remains for me a great pleasure to drive over the North Downs to Redhill every first and third Wednesday of the month for our speakers club evening.

Much of the pleasure of being a member of any speakers club is the close fellowship that forms. This is certainly the case with my membership of Redhill & Reigate. Let me briefly give one or two examples.

Chris Murphy, the current Club President, had originally joined the club a few years ago, and suffered badly from his stammer. When he returned to the club a few years later, we were immensely pleased to find that he had now become a fully confident presenter. The reason was that he had persevered very diligently with breathing exercises and with other methods of treatment of the condition during his time away, and he remains a good example to others of the way that a bad speech impediment can be improved.

Another key person within the club is Nick Rose. I had first met Nick quite a number of years before when he came along to a speaking training evening which Horsham's founder, Jim Johnston, had asked me to run in the Royal & Sun Alliance Company's premises. Although still living in Horsham, Nick became a member of the Redhill & Reigate club, served for periods as Club and Area President, and is certainly a very highly skilled speaker and evaluator.

Finally a very recent joiner has been Ian Price who transferred for convenience reasons to Redhill & Reigate from a club rather further away. Ian is a speaking trainer by profession who has been both a District President and several times a participant in National finals, including being a National Topics Winner. In his early years with ASC he had provided us with a written guide to Power Point, and had even provided South Eastern District for some years with a Power Point competition! Then, four or five years ago, he was the writer of some speaking guidebooks for ASC which were used quite widely used for a period of time.

Meanwhile, my other club – Horsham Speakers Club – was starting to rebuild. The reason why this was necessary was that in 2008 the club's President and also its Secretary had needed to leave suddenly, one for health reasons and one to return to his mother country. In addition two or three other key members had finally dropped out after several years. Our excellent new venue in Horsham's historic Tithe Barn was starting to look too spacious. It was then that my long-standing colleague Martin Jeremiah and I approached one of our newer members, Barry Miles, and asked him if he would be prepared to take over as President. He accepted, and the club once again progressed to become one of the largest in the Association.

Barry's speaking background was – and still is – both as a regular debater and as a Toastmasters member in Worthing and Brighton. He brought to the Horsham club good speaking skills, a strong commitment to the educational purpose of the speakers club, and a conscientious approach to membership growth. Since his arrival, Horsham has enjoyed a continuous flow of visitors attracted by the club website, which Barry has overseen. His spoken and email communication with all enquirers (both before and after they have made a visit), and his continuation of David Weaver's earlier initiative of sending a newsy president's letter after every meeting, is a model that other clubs would do well to adopt.

Barry was Club President for two years, and was then succeeded by Trudy Bull, also for two years. The enjoyment and the success continued. I particularly remember a meeting in which Trudy's daughter, Sabrina - a professional voice trainer - took us through numerous forms of voice exercises, which I myself have used since then at other clubs. Following Trudy, the club committee then nominated me to become Club President, and I took on that role for the two years 2012 to 2014, before handing over to Chris Hindle. Aided by a magnificent committee, that period was yet another most happy experience in my own speakers club life.

It was the membership survey 20 years previously that had shown a remarkable difference between clubs in Scotland and the North and those in the southern half of the country. Some 90% of club members in the north would attend every meeting, especially in the 'men only' clubs that were so frequent at that time. In the South, however, average attendance at each meeting was only some 50% to 60% of the club's members. This is certainly the case with Horsham Speakers Club. We have a core of around 10 who attend every meeting. But probably there will also be present some 9 or 10 'occasionals', of whom at least one person is likely to be a first-timer. The number of full members typically grows from, say, a dozen in September to around 30 by the time that we break up for the summer recess (and of course icebreaker speeches are also frequent!).

In view of this pattern, one of the key figures is the person manning the Welcome Desk, who for some years was normally our treasurer Angus, and guests' comments are also a programme item at the end of each meeting. Another most important feature of the club is the fact that the speeches and evaluations are videoed (thanks especially to member Mandy Wallace, who is another who is a member both of ASC and Toastmasters), and the disc of his or her speech or evaluation is available for a £1 pound cost to the speaker. We owe too a huge debt to our refreshment supremo, Mariki, who is also the organiser of our annual dinner.

There is one further reason for the continuing strength of the club. This is the structure of its programme. Each meeting will have 3 or 4 speeches in the first half. For the second half, a topics session takes place in one meeting out of two, whilst the other meeting will have something "special". This may for instance be the club contest evening, or something more tutorial (but always participative) such as an evaluation workshop. At other times it may be a debate, a Cogers evening, an outside speaker, or perhaps a mock trial or mock wedding.

All of these factors combine to make a lively, large and well contented club which on several occasions has won the South Eastern District's "Ace of Clubs" annual trophy. I only wish that all clubs could be as well-grounded and successful as the Horsham Speakers Club.

As I mentioned earlier, there are now only these two speakers clubs in the South Area of South Eastern District. This means that the activities that play such a regular part in speakers club life, such as visits to other clubs and area seminars, rarely take place. An attempt to start a club in Dorking looked very positive initially. A Redhill & Reigate club member was running the Dorking area's business exhibition. He suggested that a Dorking speakers club could be started and indicated that he would be pleased to organise such a club. In fact he provided a table in the exhibition and arranged for me to give a talk about the idea. Interest was certainly present. Unfortunately the would-be setter-upper for various reasons took it no further, and no club was started. Such unfortunately is life!

Moving on to wider issues, it was, I believe, originally the Church of England which is said to have realised the importance of holding events at three levels. In their case, there is the service in one's local church, a combined service bringing several local churches together, and finally an occasional grander service for celebration for the whole of the Bishopric or wider region. ASC is similar. We have the club meeting, which I have just described. Then the meetings for Area and District, which take place annually, and are events which I attend and enjoy. Finally we also need one or more national celebration events.

For me, a highlight of the year continues to be my attendance at ASC's National Conference, no longer as an NEC member, but just as a club member. It is a time to renew friendships. Some features of the weekend can change from year to year. There may or may not be a Friday evening entertainment theme; there may or may not be a partners outing on the Saturday; there may or may not be any development or education seminars. Regardless of this, the annual dinner which welcomes the incoming National President remains outstanding, the contests remain at times breathtaking, and – for we longer term members – the annual meeting of General Council remains full of absorbing interest.

Some conferences stand out, and perhaps I can briefly reminisce. Cardiff in 2012 was one of these, due to some unusual features. For example there was an 'open mic' session, and also an invitation to play and select the musical accompaniment to the dinner. We also had the stirring presence of a Welsh Male Voice Choir prior to that dinner.

The 2013 conference stood out for me for a different reason. That reason was a seminar led by Robert and Lis Hill which described some actions of Angus County Council in association with ASC. The Council had cottoned on to the great relevance of ASC speaking training to their own situation, especially when it concerned structuring presentations. Thus, with ASC's help, their staff were able to prepare speeches and had opportunities to give topics, partly within their own employment hours. This did not quite reach that level of an in-house ASC speakers club which, as is now starting to be realised, could be a sizeable opportunity for ASC. However it scored highly as "soft PR" for ASC and its local clubs.

The period leading up to the 2014 conference also stands out in my memory, though for a rather different reason. I received a call from Western District's Susan Trafford who had the task of putting together a development seminar for the conference, and was startled to find that she was totally unaware of the existence of that medium-term strategy which had been developed and fully agreed a few years previously. How could this be the case? As discussions proceeded, it became very clear that the medium-term strategy and methods which had been so carefully created had not been revised, updated, nor even used, but rather had simply been put on a shelf and forgotten. Susan herself grasped immediately that there was an element of "reinventing the wheel" in now putting on a development seminar to generate some ideas. Nevertheless she created and ran an enjoyable seminar at Conference and later wrote this up in a helpful report.

Looking at the situation from a wider perspective, a Mike Douse email which I saw at about that time put it more starkly: "I have long been concerned about the lack of continuity. Gwyn, for example, devoted his year to developing an ASC long term strategy which, as soon as he was out of office, did a titanic". Taking action on the strategy during those missing years would not have prevented the immense build-up of clubs by our Toastmasters competitor, but should certainly have prevented the steep decline in ASC's own clubs over that period.

From 1989, the Association was able to hold two annual celebrations: the annual National Conference, and the annual Speaker of the Year Dinner. It is unfortunate, and even tragic in my opinion, that the second great celebration of the year has now been removed from the ASC calendar. The annual Speaker of the Year Dinner gave the Association the opportunity to show off its wares and the potential to have a greater presence in the country. It also gave each of us the opportunity to meet and be inspired or entertained by a speaker of considerable distinction. The memories of these occasions – Simon Weston, Joe Simpson, Jack Webster, Sally Magnusson – the politicians, celebrities and men of the cloth – will never die away. I am certainly not alone in hoping that some future and far-sighted President will one day reinstate this great ASC tradition.

This, by the way, takes away nothing away from a new national event which has emerged. I refer to the concept of the National President's Dinner. This would appear to be becoming an annual occasion not only to meet up but also to hear remarkable speeches from some of ASC's own greatest talents. I very much enjoyed the Dinner hosted by National President Margaret Robertson in Glasgow 2014, and I am certainly looking forward to this year's event, which will be held by National President William Warren in Oxford in the autumn of this year, 2015.

I should also make brief mention of another initiative which recently caught my eye. This is the concept of ASC members in some way choosing the best speech or speeches of the year by a well-known national figure. It will be interesting to see how this develops, but meanwhile my own 35 year speaking journey now includes one extra happening each year. This is the Panaputti Weekend.

It was former National President Eric Taylor, I believe, who first began this new addition to the diary. I recall Eric primarily because for some years, as well as editing The Speaker, he had videoed the speakers in the final of the National Speech Contest, and these videos were available for us to buy should we wish to do so. He was then elected as National President and, sometime after handing over to his successor a year later, he founded the Panapputi Club. (The name stands for PAst-NAt-Presidents, by the way!). In this "club", past National Presidents and their partners meet up for one weekend a year in a hotel in some interesting part of the country. The programme includes a trip to a local attraction and especially dinner on the Saturday evening. In recent years for example we have visited the Durham museum town of Beamish, the Britannia yacht near Edinburgh, and the new docklands area of Liverpool. The event, which of course we pay for ourselves, is organised by one or two "volunteers" and, I am pleased to say, has only two rules. One is that we should wear our 'Purple Tie' (awarded to us at the end of our term of office) at the Saturday evening dinner. The other rule is that we must not discuss ASC matters. The first is easy to keep – the second rule much harder!

So where have we got to? Thus far this has been a "looking back" memoir covering my time in ASC, and I certainly have much to look back on. Perhaps I should do some summarising at this point before I go on to the future and also to the many wider aspects of my speaking journey which have developed.

I have a strong feeling that if you are around for long enough (which in my cases is now approaching 35 years), you eventually get around to doing everything. This is certainly true in my case, since it has included:

starting several clubs
running various courses
organising a National Conference and a Speaker of the Year gala dinner
being a national speech finalist and serving various stints as District President, and one as National President.

The highlights have been many. It is a highlight every time I see a new person come on board and grow into a fulfilled new speaker. It is a highlight when I see a new evaluator analyse a speech and encourage the speaker. But if I were to pull out just my three most interesting moments in ASC, they are all from my early days and are:

- being District President at the time when we hosted the visit of Moscow Speakers Club
- drafting out the present District structure when I was a member of the NEC's Development Committee
- and carrying out the major market research survey back in the 80s

And what have I personally got out of ASC? The first and most obvious benefit is that it enabled me to become a confident speaker and carry out the speaking part of my business life, which was the reason for which I had originally joined. In other words, ASC "did what it said on the can". But I could go on much beyond that. There are the long and close friendships. There is the pleasure of listening and the continuous stimulation that it has given. There is the pleasure that speaking itself gives. There have been the excellent opportunities for helping in every way from running events and courses to giving tutorials and evaluations. Finally there is the great interest of being involved for 35 years at different levels in a very worthwhile movement.

It is indeed a long time since Tom Williams first mentioned the arrival of a speakers club in the town where I lived, and I was persuaded to visit it. However my ASC life continues to be highly enjoyable, and I hope that I have been able to convey some of my enjoyment in these chapters.

And the future?

It is apparent that the earlier dream of colonising the whole country with ASC's speakers clubs from coast-to-coast was just that – a dream. The dormant competitor has returned with huge impact. The growth plans we created so carefully have not been heeded or used. Also, as Debra Owen Hughes once wrote during her time as National Development Officer, so much depends on the energy and enthusiasm of those who are elected to hold office at all the levels of ASC. "It feels at times like trying to push treacle uphill" were her actual words. The number of clubs has reduced by one third since 1990, and the number of club members by over half. I was particularly sad to hear that the speakers club in which I first set foot, Cheltenham Speakers Club, had dropped to just three or four members and was thinking of closing.

I sense, however, that in 2015 as I write down these memoirs, there is a certain optimism in the air. New people are coming to the fore. New plans are being developed. Importantly these include plans for utilising social media, which have emerged only in the last few years and are a vital force. Activity includes the "Renaissance" drive led by recent past National Presidents Graham McLachlan and Lindsay Dutch, the social media initiative and other development work led by South Eastern District's Paul Johnstone, and the various seminars to be held in Oxford on the day of the forthcoming President's Dinner. Under the leadership of National President William Warren, there is more of a willingness for change management or, as a translation of the Italian poet Lampedusa puts it, "If we don't want things to change, things will have to change". It is not just planning, but being an organisation that carries through its plans, which has to be the new message, and I have confidence that much will be achieved.

William Warren (ASC National President) and Suzanne at the Association's 2015 National Conference in Southport

To return to my own speaking story, there is a well-known piece of advice to would-be speakers which goes as follows: "Finish speaking before your audience has finished listening". Perhaps the same applies to writing. In other words "Finish writing before your readers have finished wishing to read". However, as touched upon once or twice in these chapters, my speaking journey has spread much more widely outside ASC in these last few years. This memoir of my speaking journey would be incomplete were I not to give, in shorter summary form, some details of these wider interests and where they have led me. I invite you to carry on reading for one final chapter.

Chapter 8

My Speaking Journey expands

I mentioned at an earlier stage of this book a letter which I received in 1994 regarding another style of speaking, and the meeting which I attended as a result. My own personal speaking journey since that time has extended to bodies well beyond ASC, and has embraced debating as well as speaking. It would be totally wrong not to include details of some of these in a book entitled "My Speaking Journey". So here goes with the first of these bodies – the Cogers.

Society of Cogers

The letter that I received in 1994 was from Magnus Nielsen regarding the Society of Cogers who in those days were meeting on a Saturday evening in the Betsey Trotwood pub in Clerkenwell. At that time, although it sounded interesting, I was unable to attend. It was 3 years later, in 1997, that I happened to hear that Magnus Nielsen would be running a Cogers demonstration evening at the Insurance Institute of London Speakers Club, and I decided to attend.

The Society of Cogers was founded in 1755 in the City of London as one of the coffee house debating clubs that were quite popular at that time. The Cogers is the only one that has lasted right up to the present, and its historical records are held in the Guildhall Library in London. It can justifiably claim to be the oldest free speech speaking club in the world. In strict semantic terms, it is more of a discussion club than a debating club. Chaired by an officer called "The Grand", the meeting starts with an "Opener" who runs through the events of the last month for a quarter of an hour or so. Following this, all present are invited to give their own thoughts on any events of the month for up to 5 minutes. In its present form – and instituted by Magnus – the meeting then ends with an "Evaluator" who comments on the speaking and awards the Apple (of Discord!) to one of those who have spoken

It was an excellent meeting. What I found particularly stimulating was that the current affairs subject matter naturally included discussions relating to religion, politics and sex which are frowned upon in ASC speakers clubs. This of course led to lively but still very friendly confrontations during the evening. Hence at the close of the meeting I, together with Alex Young and Neville White, who were senior Insurance Institute Speakers Club members, urged Magnus very strongly to set up a Cogers Society which would meet somewhere in the City on a weekday evening. We promised to underwrite the venture for 6 months if necessary. Magnus was happy to do this, and the first meeting of the newly formed City of London Society of Cogers took place in the cellar of the Jamaica Wine Bar, off Cornhill in the City, late in 1997. It was a success right from the start. A small committee was formed, a website and mailing list were put in hand, and the monthly meeting schedule was announced.

We soon discovered that Magnus harboured a dream. This was that Cogers clubs should proliferate around the country, just as the "Café Philosophes" movement had spread throughout France. The dream was unfortunately never realised, but it did lead to the decision to found a Cogers Trust which could have a central role in such a development. For this purpose, we adopted the wording of a charitable AIDS trust (the Friends of Chilonga) which I had chaired for several years, and we duly registered the Cogers Trust. For the stated objective, which needs to be present in the formation of such a trust, we decided upon "education in public speaking" as our purpose.

It has been an exhilarating 18 years since those early days, even though Magnus's original vision of a widespread national movement failed to develop. Cogers societies meet regularly in the City of London, the City of Westminster, and in the Hertfordshire town of Ware. There is also a slight link with the San Francisco Cogers, which is an old established gentleman's luncheon club founded by some earlier English expatriates. Members of Cogers societies range from university students to the retired, and from anarchists right through to a UKIP parliamentary candidate. In addition several ASC clubs in the south-east have included a Cogers meeting as a one-off event in their meeting programme.

The normal pattern is that Cogers clubs hold a standard meeting once a month. However over the years various special events have taken place. For instance we were once able to hold a Cogers meeting in a committee room in the Palace of Westminster, whilst not surprisingly we have also held a Cogers meeting at Speakers Corner in Hyde Park. The year 2005 was the 250th anniversary of the foundation of the original Society of Cogers, so we marked it by several events. One of these was a Speaking Olympiad. A total of 4 teams participated – a Cogers team, a speakers club team, a Kingston Debating Society team, and a Rotary "Youth Speaks" team. Thus there were 4 styles of speaking present, and each team had to undertake all the styles. For example the speakers club style was Table Topics, and the debating society style was a Proposer speech and an Opposer speech.

For personal reasons, one of the most significant evenings for me was a special meeting which we held in the function room of the nearby Devereux pub fairly soon after the 9/11 attack on the Twin Towers. The title of the meeting was "Liberty vs Security – What is the Balance?" To lead the Cogers discussion on that occasion, we had invited broadcaster Claire Fox, who was later to establish the Institute of Ideas, and a senior contingency planning manager, David Kerry, who became a keen Cogers member and is now a Trustee of the Cogers Trust. The arguments put forward were very soundly constructed, but it was the arrival of an unexpected attendee which marked the event for me.

This unexpected visitor was a certain Mark Covell (normally known to friends simply as 'Sky'). He had returned a day or two before from Genoa where – along with 57 others – he had been the victim of severe night-time violence by the Italian police, in return for having been a G8 protester. In Mark's case, this included fractured ribs, missing teeth and two days in a coma in a Genoa hospital. His only "crime" had been that of being a journalist and web expert with the non-corporate Indymedia organisation. He and I quite soon became close friends. Over the next 10 years (yes, Italian justice really did take that long!) I was able to be of assistance whilst the 57 were fighting their case through the Italian courts and eventually gaining very sizeable compensation. Those years also included such interesting episodes as visits with Mark to Parliaments in Brussels and Rome and, of course, several times to Genoa. I even found myself chairing a widely-attended "From Genoa to

Guantánamo" conference in the Conway Hall in which one of my speakers was the first Britisher to have been released after several years imprisoned in Guantánamo Bay!

Meantime the Cogers Trust has continued to play its strong part in the London debating scene. One popular initiative has been the creation of an annual Eastbourne Debating Conference which has been held every October for the last five years. This is a joint event with the Sylvans and with Debating London (see details later). The weekend includes 3 debates (i.e. one in each of our styles), 2 workshops and a special dinner which may well include a balloon debate. The Alexandra Hotel in Eastbourne is most welcoming and, needless to say, this event is proving most popular.

Sylvan Debating Club

It was through the Cogers that I first became aware of the Sylvan Debating Club, commonly known as 'The Sylvans'. It was Cogers member Donald Leon Soon, a fellow-Trustee of the Cogers, who first introduced me. The year was about 2000.

The Sylvans had been founded in 1868 by a member of the Harmsworth family, and the current Lord Harmsworth is still a Trustee of the club. In the words of the Official History, the club's inception was a discussion "on top of one of the Green Atlas buses which ran from the City through Baker Street and the Abbey Road to the Prince of Wales Hotel in St John's Wood". The Sylvans meeting format is the traditional one of a Motion, speeches by a Proposer and Opposer, speeches from the floor, final statements, and a Vote. That same Official History of the club showed great numbers attending in the late Victorian and Edwardian times. However by the time that I first attended, membership had reduced to less than a dozen, including one who was highly eccentric in everything from clothing to opinions and behaviour!

I enjoyed very much the debates that were held, decided to become a member and within 4 or 5 years took my turn as Club President for a year.

The difficulty for the Sylvans was not merely the low numbers but also the advancing age of these few members, and membership dwindled further.

Our meetings at that time were held in the Conway Hall in Red Lion Square, Holborn, which is still a renowned venue best known for its Quaker and Ethical Society connections. Room hire costs proved onerous for that small number, and the future of the Sylvans began to look doubtful. There was however a solution, and the Cogers Trust assisted.

By this time, the City of London Cogers had become established in the Old Bank of England pub in Fleet Street, next to the Law Courts. Most unusually for London, no charge was made by the pub for the side room in which we held our meeting. Presumably it was felt better to have a dozen or two potential drinkers in that room on a Monday evening on a regular basis, rather than leaving it empty. The landlord was prepared to offer that same arrangement to the Sylvans, also on a Monday, and the Sylvans' room hire problem was thereby solved.

In addition the still strongly-independent Sylvans agreed to be brought under the Cogers' wing for publicity purposes. This extended to website management and design, and to being featured in the CogersAnnounce email list of several hundred people. Sylvans numbers rapidly rose. This was also to the benefit of the Cogers who could now feature traditional debating as well as the Cogers debating style in their offerings.

It was also at about that time that the Sylvans adopted a new policy for the choice of debate subjects. This was to have Motions that were (i) topical, (ii) of importance and (iii) that had good arguments on both sides. Thus we normally find ourselves in stimulating argument on subjects such as coalitions, immigration, policing or even God.

The only exceptions to that policy are the debate at the Sylvans annual dinner and the Sylvans debate in the annual Eastbourne Conference, where a light-hearted motion seems more appropriate. As an example, the Motion in Eastbourne in 2014 was "that London should be independent", which was Proposed – and won! – by my son, Adrian (…. or could that proposal perhaps be seen as serious rather than light-hearted?).

To my and others' great pleasure, the Sylvan Debating Club continues to flourish in today's London debating scene, and I personally am most fortunate to be a long-standing committee member of this institution.

Debating and debating clubs are a long established tradition in this country. I first experienced the practice of good debating in the Cambridge Union, though I unfortunately did not participate. From time to time it had cropped up in my speakers club life. For example, Croydon Speakers Club used to hold a debate about once a year with Purley Debating Club. The arrival of Mike Douse into the speakers club scene brought debating into more prominence, since he created an ASC handbook on the subject. He himself had had considerable experience during his years in Australia, where his name lingers on in the name of the Douse Trophy which is awarded for an annual debating event for schools in which, surprisingly, one or two prisons also participate. (Could this be as a form of escape, I wonder, or could it be to show the courage of their convictions?) Armed with the experience of Cogers and Sylvans debating, and reinforced by the content of Mike's book I have now even had, by invitation, the experience of running debating evenings in both the Arun and the Guildford Toastmasters clubs as well as in my own two ASC clubs.

My own participation, however, had always been in the traditional style of debating where, after the Proposer(s) and the Opposer(s) have had their say, the others in the meeting would be invited to put forward their thoughts for a few minutes. In recent years there has been considerable development of debating in both schools and universities based on a different principle. In this style, a team of two or perhaps three on one side (the Proposition) competes against a team on the other side (the Opposition), whilst the role of the audience can be described as 'cross examination' of the two sides, rather than giving their own speeches. Over the years I had occasionally been invited to be a judge in such a contest, despite my inexperience in participating. The points are awarded for argument skill, including rebuttals, and only to a very minor extent for speaking skill. But my debating life was now to widen, largely due to a young and enterprising graduate of Greek ancestry.

Central London Debating Society

It was in 2009 that my Cogers colleague Paul Carroll mentioned to me a new organisation, the Central London Debating Society, which was holding meetings upstairs in the Harcourt Arms pub between Baker Street and Edgware

Road. I made contact and started to go along. It had been started by Tony Koutsoumbos, who was a fairly recent graduate from Nottingham University. An interesting feature was that the decision on the actual Motion to be debated was sometimes left to the very last minute, and I occasionally found myself "volunteering" to take part as one of the opening speakers. It was all good practice.

The Central London Debating Society's popularity grew strongly as did its social media database. The venture soon needed to move to a larger location, and eventually settled in the Old Cock Tavern in Fleet Street. Debate training became a feature, and one or two new offshoots were also set up. I myself began to enjoy the company of a number of new friends, who, like Tony, had left university only a very short time before.

It helped that Tony and I had other interests in common. Initially these were our political interests where we had the same UK party affiliation and also felt similarly on European issues. It was only a matter of time before we shared a further interest. This was the Eastbourne Conference, where Tony became the third member of the planning team. With the participation of the Central London Debating Society, alongside the Cogers and the Sylvans, we were able to include three styles of debating within the weekend, and this has proved popular from the start. But then, during the 2013 Eastbourne Conference came a major surprise. Out of the blue, I received from Tony an invitation to be part of a debate training team that would shortly spend two weeks of December in the East African country of Rwanda.

Rwanda is known throughout the world for one tragic episode. This was the appalling genocide which had taken place in 1994. The majority Hutu people were encouraged (even on their nation's radio!) to slaughter the minority Tutsi people, and 800,000 killings took place while the rest of the world stood by. Now, almost a score of years later, a new generation of Rwandan students were determined that this should not happen again. In the year 2000, a 20-year vision of Rwanda's future had been launched by the government, to be realised by 2020, and convincing by argument rather than by violence should be way of achieving it.

The need was for critical reasoning skills. Thus, one year previously, a small team of Rwandan recent school-leavers had started an organisation called Idebate Rwanda. Their goal was the empowerment of the next generation through debate to avoid repeating the mistakes of their predecessors. The group had been successful in providing a platform for young people to express themselves, but lacked the expertise to train them in how to have mature debates about complex public policy issues

One of these far-sighted individuals was Rwandan student, Sam Baker, who had actually been following the Central London Debating Society and its training hints online for two or three years. He then enrolled in the LSE to study Economics in London, and made contact with Tony on his second day here. Sam asked Tony if he would be willing to put a team of debate trainers together to fly out to Rwanda to run their first annual debate camp. Tony agreed, planning started, and now – with time running short and the last place still unfilled – during the Eastbourne conference of 2013, I was approached and asked if I would be one of that team.

One of the many advantages of retirement is not having to put daily work commitments first. Thus I was immediately able and delighted to accept Tony's invitation. Preparations went swiftly ahead. A whistlestop fundraising tour of four events in nine days, plus a welcome donation of £500 from CoPS, succeeded in reaching the £2500 funding target, and a team of 4 of us booked the long flight to Kigali in Rwanda. Apart from Tony and myself, the other two team members were Jack Watling, who had a post with Reuters, and Jordan Anderson, an American, who had an excellent reputation on the university debating circuit. Jordan was then working in the US Embassy in Grosvenor Square but has now become a political risk analyst specialising in the Great Lakes region of East Africa.

I could write at great length about what transpired, and indeed wrote a few hundred words of report. Can I refer those readers who may be interested to the website reference www.redgers.com/gwyn.html which includes both my report and a film of our trip. Meanwhile let me include here just a very brief summary of what was for me a once-in-a-lifetime adventure. Rwanda, by the way, was originally a small German colony in East Africa, and then a Belgian colony, which became independent in the 70s. Sometime after the 1994 genocide, the country joined the British Commonwealth and in 2009, most unusually, adopted the English language.

From the visitor's perspective, Rwanda was everything that one would expect a developing sub-Saharan nation to be. Often referred to as "the land of a thousand hills", outside its few main towns we found it to be a territory of rich and colourful vegetation but also of subsistence farming and still considerable poverty. However there was also the beginnings of a small but developing middle-class, and it was from this that a secondary school system had been established.

The place where we were going to teach was a pioneering two-week "Debate Camp" for young people from 15 to 22, held mainly in the Gashora Girls School of Science and Technology, an hour or two from the capital, Kigali, which had been founded by two American philanthropists after the genocide. Well over a hundred students were attending, and we divided these between the four of us. It was a full and busy two weeks of tuition and finally of competitions, and proved both demanding and enjoyable. Probably my strongest abiding memory is of the warmth, vibrancy and sheer ability of those students. I can only hope that we were able to give to them as much as they gave to us! (In practice, this was possibly achieved. They have since received structured funding from the UN, and three of them have secured scholarships in the USA largely as a result.)

The venture was much appreciated, and a slightly larger team was invited for the following December also. I myself did not return, but know that the expedition once again proved highly successful, and that Rwandan schools debating is now very much on the international map.

Meanwhile, back in this country, the activities of the Central London Debating Society – or of 'Debating London' which it was soon to become – continued apace. I attended when my own diary allowed. Vauxhall's Tea House Theatre became the venue for many regular debates, and turned out to be an excellent choice. Another successful venue was the Quaker Meeting House in Leicester Square which was used for 'Friday Night Soapbox', and debate training events took place in other venues also.

The schedule was in fact becoming quite demanding. Tony and his colleague Jason shared the running of Debating London. A further group of post-university personnel – Shaughan, Charlotte and others – were avid supporters and champions of the group (and assisted with Debate Camp Rwanda), whilst at the same time pursuing their own careers. However it was fairly clear that Tony might eventually have to make a decision. His debating interests were extremely time-consuming. Could he in fact make a career out of debating or should he follow another main path as a career choice?

In the meantime, and while still undecided, he continued to forge ahead. For practical purposes, he created a trust – the Debating Foundation – of which three of his supporters – Paul Carroll, Vince Stevenson and I – became Trustees. This would in time facilitate receiving funding for the debate training work that he was increasingly carrying out for community projects in the East End of London. Then a further step followed, namely the Great Debaters Club, which was a business that brought together different strands of his activity – the regular debates, the debate training activity, a link with some commercial debating events, involvement in the annual Eastbourne Debating Conference, and so on. Its financial basis was started through a crowdfunding method and there, as I write, the situation stands today.

All of us now look forward to further developments in this remarkable story, but meanwhile let me turn to another discovery which I made – the Simpletons Speakers Club.

Simpletons Speakers Club

There have long been a handful of speakers clubs that have remained independent from ASC or from Toastmasters. An example from my Cheltenham days was a club at Bristol, and one from my Croydon days was a club at Woking. The London-based Simpletons Speakers Club was another which I greatly enjoyed until its closure a year or two ago

It was started about 40 years previously by people who had attended a lively Speaking in Management (SIM) training course – hence the rather off-putting title "The Simpletons Club". I was first introduced to the Simpletons by one or two contacts in, I believe, the year 2002. I later joined the club and remained as a fairly regular attendee until the club's demise in 2013.

One of the reasons for making my monthly trip to the upstairs function room of a Paddington tavern was the opportunity to meet and mix with a variety of members, extending from some who were members of the Professional Speakers Association (PSA) at one end down to complete novices at the other end. But perhaps a more important reason was the variety of the programme schedule. We might have a training session from, say, a professional drama coach, or hold a dinner to give us experience in after-dinner speeches. At other times the programme might consist of a debate or a spoken poetry evening. I recall with great pleasure a session which was devoted largely to learning how to compose and then deliver limericks.

Especially noteworthy were the meetings for which we were challenged to imagine ourselves in totally unfamiliar situations. The task for one of these was to compose a perfect fraud. This produced some most thoughtful results from the most law-abiding people. In fact it led me to wonder why I had followed my own marketing career for so many years when an activity that included sending a letter from a Nigerian post-box address might have better feathered my nest. An even more challenging task was to create and deliver a eulogy. I decided that I should write my own eulogy which I might possibly deliver from within that box, positioned there in front of the congregation. After all, I felt, I was the reason for their coming along to that place at that time, so why should I not be permitted to have my say?

The Simpletons were always prepared to be sociable, and another strong memory was the presence of a "Simpletons Table" at ASC's Speaker of the Year dinner for Digby Jones. That name needed some explanation to my ASC colleagues! But unfortunately many good things come to an end, and one of these was the Simpletons Speakers Club, so I shall now move on to talk about another organisation which will hopefully continue for years to come.

Speakers Trust

The original Speakers Trust – or, to give it its full name, the Andrew Ducker Speakers Trust – was established by two ASC club members and two Toastmasters club members shortly before I joined Croydon Speakers Club. The Trust was founded to commemorate a speakers club member who had sadly died at too young an age. One of these four founders was Croydon

Speakers Club member, Peter Curtis-Allen. The Speakers Trust had remained a small charity. Its main activity had been to support several speakers clubs by providing them with a trophy that they could use for a club purpose. However Peter himself was quite ambitious for the charity to grow and assist more ASC and Toastmasters clubs.

Peter had another string to his bow. His own profession was IT or, more specifically, the ownership of Net Services International which was in fact the host for the ASC website during its first years, including a full listing and map of all the speakers clubs in the country. It was through this venture that Peter came to work closely with ASC's Webmaster, Keir Smart. At the same time he had developed a close relationship with Toastmasters District Governor, David Thompson who, more than any other person, was responsible for the rebirth and rapid growth of the Toastmaster movement in the UK from the 90s onward. Both Keir and David became Trustees of the Speakers Trust. Peter was particularly proud that he had thereby established the first positive contact between the two organisations since the rupture of 30 years previously.

Two or three years later, to the Trustees' surprise, Speakers Trust was approached by the recently established Speakers Bank. This was a training venture, founded by Sue Warner who had links with both Toastmasters and ASC. Its purpose was to bring speaking training free of charge to groups such as children, the unemployed, and others who would not normally be in a position to afford training or club fees. Thanks to the lively management of Jez Sweetland, it had rapidly become a very large venture indeed. However Speakers Bank did not have charitable status, which was virtually essential for developing its mix of activities further. The purpose of the approach to Speakers Trust was to try and gain the status. Following discussion, the very small Speakers Trust therefore agreed that the several times larger Speakers Bank would become its subsidiary, thus solving the latter's charitable status problem.

Keir eventually resigned his position as a Trustee and, in 2005, I was invited by Peter to become a Trustee of the Speakers Trust. I had come to view the Trust as the speaking world's charity, and thus a venture to be supported by those of us in that world. Moreover, with the recent addition of Speakers Bank, the Trust now had a very large and exciting potential indeed for carrying out speech training work (through its expert trainers such as ASC's Michael Ronayne) amongst all kinds of deserving groups. I was therefore most pleased to accept the invitation to be a Trustee.

The most developed activity of the Trust had become – and in 2015 still remains – the Jack Petchey Organisation's annual schools speaking contest. Jack Petchey himself, now very elderly, was an East Ender who had built up a massive property construction business and was now putting his wealth to great use for the benefit of the youth of Greater London and Essex. Via his organisation's financial contribution, all state secondary schools within Greater London and Essex are entitled to have a full day's speaking tuition for some of their Year 5 pupils, and also participate in a series of local and regional contests that culminate in a truly remarkable "Final" each year, with judges drawn from fields such as MPs and the professional and cultural worlds.

Interestingly, the success and popularity of the Jack Petchey contest was probably the main reason why, a few years ago, the BBC launched its own television contest to find the "Young Speaker of the Year". Speakers Bank's Sean Kennedy, who had largely built up the Jack Petchey contest, was the programme's Speaking Consultant. I was fortunate enough to be able to attend the final celebration party of the BBC series, and talk to the producer and two or three of the celebrities and others who had taken part in different stages. All agreed that it had been a success. Nevertheless, and to my and others' disappointment, the series was not repeated.

My own role as a Trustee was most interesting from every angle.

One early task for the Trustees was to develop a more suitable structure. The disparity in size was regularised two or three years later by the very large subsidiary, Speakers Bank, changing its name to Speakers Trust and taking over the charitable status whilst the original and very small Speakers Trust was discontinued. The changes also involved some additional trustee strength. This was at a time when, due to the ASC Speaker of the Year connection, I was in fairly close touch with (Lord) Digby Jones. With the agreement of our fellow Trustees, Sue Warner and I visited him at the House of Lords, and he agreed to become the Speakers Trust President for a period of time. Also as part of our strengthening, I was especially pleased that we were able to welcome ASC's

Gwyneth Millard as the ASC's nominee to become a Trustee.

A particularly memorable occasion, which we were able to use to launch the recently renamed Speakers Trust, was a reception in Speakers House. Our host on that occasion was The Speaker himself, John Bercow MP, and his wife and family were also present. The venue was outstanding. After all we were having this reception in a set of rooms which had recently cost the British taxpayer over £25,000 for new wallpaper! I was particularly pleased that ASC's then President Joe James, as well as Gwyneth Millard and I, were able to be present for this memorable event.

The marketing challenge for Speakers Trust was interesting, and occupied much of my time initially. The task was twofold. Firstly to develop the brand and the potential client base such as, for instance, a speaking training scheme amongst recently released prisoners in the Midlands. Secondly, since we were a charity rather than a commercial company, to help in identifying fund-raising or "donor" opportunities. One result of our work was the creation of a "Speaking in the Community" package, whilst other results included some projects brought in to us by individual trainers.

Of especial interest to me were aspects concerning the link between ASC and the Speakers Trust. I have always held the view that the development of links with outside bodies can be of great benefit to ASC in its own development. In this case, being close to Speakers Trust would be of advantage to ASC both in having a charitable link that we could mention, and also possibly in club development. After all, Speakers Trust in its original form had provided some small donations to several ASC clubs, and the prospects for mutual benefit were very real.

One of the disappointments of my speaking journey is that these possible benefits were not realised. Following a change of management, the Speakers Trust preferred to move away from a strong link with speakers clubs. I therefore had a choice to make – to continue or not to continue. It was with regret that I decided to stand down from being a Trustee since linking the Trust with speakers clubs was possibly my main interest. Instead I would concentrate on the other demanding aspects of my speaking and debating interests.

It was a difficult decision to make. That part of my speaking journey had been both enjoyable and challenging, and to this day I retain a keen interest in the progress of the Speakers Trust. However I still feel that I made the right decision in the circumstances.

U3A Speaking & Debating Group

Another of the great advantages of the retired life is the opportunity to be a member of the University of the Third Age. From its academic beginnings in France, the U3A was brought to this country some 25 years ago by a trio of forward thinkers, including a Fellow, Peter Laslett, of my own previous college. Within the United Kingdom, U3As now have well over half a million members and have extended their scope from purely academic learning right through to some social activities.

It was in 2005 that I finally retired, but it was only four or five years later that I decided to become a member of my local branch, which was Merton U3A. I found that almost 100 activities were offered for the amazingly low fee of £12 for a year – participation in music and the arts, studying philosophy or a new language, talks, walks, visits, and even cross-stitch and Scrabble. I was spoilt for choice, but in the end, I joined a current affairs group and an Italian conversation group, went to some monthly talks, and have remained a member ever since.

A founding philosophy of the U3A movement is that members should not merely take something out but should also, if possible, put something back in. It was therefore not too long before the thought came to me that I myself could offer an activity within this self-help environment. That activity could be either speaking or debating. In the end I decided that the best step would be to join them together as the "Merton U3A Speaking & Debating Group". After discussion, I therefore bought a lectern, announced the group's formation in the Merton U3A's website and newsletter, and went ahead. We decided to meet in the Community Centre in Colliers Wood, just south of Tooting in South London, and have continued to meet there for two hours once a fortnight. The numbers attending are small – never more than 10 – but this is to be preferred since it gives everyone ample time to speak.

Our programme has steadily evolved over the years since we began. Unlike a speakers club, the purpose of coming along is only partially to improve one's skill, and not at all to get a better job. Instead it is more often for the social reason of just spending time together, plus very often for the wish to share ideas. The member may have never talked to groups, and thus be a complete first timer. Or it may be, for the member, a continuation of an aspect of his or her earlier career and interests.

The question put to me is always the same. It is "What do you speak about?" The answer can only be "anything and everything"! The format of our sessions has evolved to become normally:

- a brief warm-up item
- talks by those present, on a theme set (informally) as homework
- impromptus around that same theme or something different
- maybe a very brief tutorial or similar activity
- discussion of issues, which can range from a mini-debate to a Cogers session, or perhaps to a BBC-style Question Time.

Just in case this sounds too formal, our get-together in the week when I am writing this – a typical meeting – went from talks about a well-known person (Chris Evans, David Beckham) to some impromptus with a gesture theme (e.g. 2 minutes on "tidying up the kitchen") and then Question Time on such issues as policy towards refugee immigrants and the best age for starting a family. And, as always, a great opportunity for a cup of tea and a natter!

When I started the group, I was totally taken aback to discover a virtually complete absence of 'speaking and debating' groups taking place in U3A branches anywhere in the country. Indeed there were no guidelines on such an activity available from the National Office in Bromley, which has copious guidelines and assistance on scores of other activities. I decided therefore, after a couple of years, to put together a document that I entitled a "Source Book" for running such an activity. In it I listed much of what we had done, such as the subjects for topics, speeches and warm-ups, the tutorial or exercise items, and the various styles of debating or discussion. . This is now available from U3A's National Office. There is still a long way to go, but I am aware that Merton's U3A is no longer the only U3A to offer its members a speaking and/or debating opportunity.

The last two or three years have seen a most interesting development in which the University of the Third Age has played an important part. This has been the holding of an "inter-generational debate" between some U3A members and some 16-17 year old school attendees. It is a joint activity, primarily organised by the English Speaking Union and the House of Lords public relations machine. On several occasions over the years, my interest in speaking had enabled me to attend a speaking event in the Houses of Parliament, who incidentally have their own debating club in conjunction with the Chartered Institute of Marketing. For example, we had been able to hold a unique Cogers session in a Committee Room, and I had even been asked to judge a speaking competition there for a political party. In addition I have had the opportunity to attend the debate events that were run by ASC's National Development Officer Debra Owen Hughes for two or three years (and thus have a treasured certificate stating that "Gwyn Redgers has spoken in the House of Commons"!). However on the occasion of these inter-generational debates, we achieved the rare distinction of being all seated on the benches in the actual House of Lords chamber, with the House of Lords Speaker (Baroness D'Souza) as the debate chairman. I hope very much that these events will continue and thrive.

At a much earlier stage of my ASC time, I had considered the possibility that there could be U3A speakers clubs within ASC itself, rather like an in-house club in a hospital or a firm. I no longer believe that this is possible but would still recommend the club to include the local U3A amongst any organisations with which it has a link. From my own point of view, it has indeed been a very rewarding part of my own speaking journey.

Finally in this record of organisations other than ASC which have played a significant role in my speaking journey, let me return to that earlier development, the College of Public Speaking, which was discussed in a previous chapter of this book.

College of Public Speaking

It will be recalled that the College of Public Speaking (or 'CoPS' which I shall call it for simplicity) was designed as a corporate training venture to run alongside ASC's clubs with a view to attracting more money to ASC and more members to its clubs. It was launched at a major business exhibition in London, and an initial mailing attracted some excellent enquiries. Unfortunately for ASC, however, as was described in that earlier chapter, doubts arose in some quarters and thus its aim of helping ASC came to an end. Nevertheless CoPS itself continued successfully, though this was now for its own benefit rather than for the benefit of ASC.

The immediate result of separating from ASC was that a change of Directors was needed. I resigned my directorship, as did Gwyneth Millard and Dilwyn Scott. Michael Ronayne and Richard Johnson agreed to be appointed and joined Vince Stevenson as the Directors of the company. I continued to hold the position of Company Secretary and in addition still continue to this day as the Financial Officer.

For the first year or two, CoPS continued its initially planned method. This was to approach the HR departments of very large employers and provide speaking training courses, ideally in the client's own premises. One of the earliest clients, which has continued to use the services of CoPS on almost a dozen occasions, was Buckingham Palace or, more specifically, the curators of the Household Collections mainly at Windsor and in Buckingham Palace itself. Gaining entry to the Palace is indeed quite a frequent journey for Michael Ronayne.

A development, which has become one of the two mainstays, was to switch to aiming at individuals rather more than at their companies. By this method, it became possible to advertise regular training days in various locations which include Arundel House and Bloomsbury House in Central London. The normal programme is now a one-day or longer course which may be basic or advanced. The greatest success has been achieved through Vince Stevenson's specific targeting of those persons who are very frightened about speaking in public, but still need to do so for their day-to-day work.

An additional development, which has also become a most important mainstay of CoPS was gaining accreditation for a Train the Trainer course. Operation of the course is now in the very accomplished hands of Michael

Ronayne, who normally runs two per month. This is a competitive market place, in which the quality of the CoPS course stands out strongly indeed.

The success of CoPS has of course required considerable marketing endeavour. For a start, our courses need to come up high on the search engine, and CoPS has always been most fortunate in having Vince, who is expert in this field. Additionally a strong reputation has been built up in London largely through development of the College of Public Speaking's annual Corporate Challenge in which both established speakers and others compete. Another venture which gained much applause for CoPS was staging a repeat of that Speaking Olympiad which had originally been put on so successfully by the Cogers.

Other links too have also helped to maintain the company's position as one of the leaders in public speaking training in the busy London marketplace. These have included close working with the Institute of the Spoken Word of Kingston University, arranged for CoPS by Mike Douse. Additionally Vince and I were invited to lunch by the leaders of the English Speaking Union, which held out the possibility of a working relationship. CoPS can therefore look forward with confidence. But nevertheless life is not all success.

An example was our intended development of a computer-based speaking training diploma. In this technological age, it makes immediate sense that the computer will come to play an important part in speaker training just as it does in other training fields. It was a major cooperative effort to undertake the development of a 12-module diploma course which could be used by would-be public speakers around the world. Regrettably the hoped-for results failed to materialise and, for the moment, further development has therefore been halted.

Another brake to the firm's progress occurred when one of the three directors – Richard Johnson – needed to withdraw from his training role in CoPS in order to pursue his own academic career away from London. It was Richard who originally built up the strategy of providing day courses for individuals rather than for companies, and he has been missed. Thus as I write these notes, CoPS has a high income, but consists primarily of two highly talented trainers, Vince Stevenson and Michael Ronayne, each pursuing his own training practice. The question of developing it on to the next level – possibly extending away from London – possibly having more management or sales strength – possibly widening its range to be more "collegiate" – remains on the table.

The Final Word

In conclusion, within the pages of this book I have attempted to recount my own speaking journey, originally just with the Association of Speakers Clubs but also, for the last 18 years, with a wider spread of organisations. It has been – and still remains – a most exhilarating journey.

I thank you, dear reader, for staying the course and for sharing the story of that journey with me. I trust that it has been of interest and, most importantly, I trust that your own speaking journey is – or will be – equally memorable.

Gwyn Redgers, July 2015